Poetry Magic:
Our Voice of Healing

Kelly Mullins

ISBN: 979-8-9872840-0-1

Please visit https://knownotknow.me

Contact via email: Warrior.Poet.KMullins@gmail.com

This book is dedicated to:
Peace, Logan, Lawson, and Xanni
You have all taught me what it
feels like to Love unconditionally.

To Boomer,
for showing me what it feels like to
be loved unconditionally.

Table of Contents

Introduction

Greetings

You already know that everything is energy: from a mustard seed to two black holes colliding. Thoughts are energy. Emotions are energy. Trauma... is energy.

Healing is energy!

This is what magic is.
This is what poetry is.

I am so grateful for this opportunity to share with you how poetry has been such a powerful healing energy in my life. But let's back up a step and talk about magic first.

When you think of magic, do you think of slight-of-hand, smoke and mirrors and creepy dudes stabbing attractive women with swords? Or, do you think of wizards calling earthquakes and fire to slay giant demon-beasts? Or maybe you are a witch and value the flow of energy in nature.

These are all magic. You see, magic is the very essence of creativity. And creativity is the most powerful energy we have at our control. Focused through the lens of poetry, that energy can quite literally work miracles! And the thing is, you don't have to believe in magic to create it!

So let this book be your conduit into the dimension of Poetry Magic. Let it be your book of spells. Here, you will no longer write poetry, you will cast Poetry like magic spells.

About this Book

There are six chapters in this book, covering different elements of Poetry Magic. Each chapter opens with a brief intro discussing how the poems within can heal. At the end of each chapter, there is a discussion in which we explore the topic a bit more. I'll provide personal anecdotes on how I've experienced healing related to the topic.

To me, the real healing begins when poetry is a shared experience. This is why I take every chance I can to share my poetry in a microphone in front of people. That shared experience means that I don't heal alone, and the power of the magic is exponentially multiplied.

And I very much want to have that shared experience with you, in this book. So at the end of the discussion session, I will give you a writing prompt based on the subject matter of the chapter, and you will have a couple pages to write your own magical healing poem. If those pages are not enough, there are more at the end of the book.

It would **fill my entire being** with gratitude and joy to receive photos of those poems in my inbox:
warrior.poet.kmullins@gmail.com.

About Me
I don't want to talk about me, but I will because it makes sense. I've experienced more trauma than the average person. I have been living with mental illness most of my life. I've also been writing poetry most of my life. I have a degree in English-Writing. I have performed/read poetry into a bunch of microphones, in front of a bunch of crowds big and small; I've also read poetry across countless tables in cafes, restaurants, and picnic tables. Poetry has helped me through an enormous amount of difficulties. First, putting the words on a page, then sharing it. This is where the magic happened. If I had to define what Poetry Magic was in two words, it would be: create & share.

I truly hope you enjoy this book. If you have the desire to reach out, please feel free to email me.

From the depths of my being, Thank you!
~Kelly Mullins

Invocation of Goddess Brigid

Goddess of Poetry, Goddess of Healing hear this prayer.
Fill us with your Love and whisper into our hearts that
your words may blanket the pages to come with
beauty and wisdom.

Help us heal ourselves that we may become
beacons of healing for all living beings.
Dwell within this sacred House
we build that all travelers
may find the respite
of your hearth...

This House

Welcome weary Traveler to this
    House of Rest.
Your voice may feel like the dust of desert roads
    and your words may feel as if they
fall from your lips to the floor
    shattering silently.
Know that here you have a voice, and
    to us it sounds like gentle, soothing music.
To us it sounds like cool rain beneath brutal summer suns.
To us it sounds like shade from a wise old oak –
    secrets free to all who wish to hear.
We wish to hear you.
We have been waiting for you.
We are happy to finally know you.
So speak here in this House and
    feel replenished.

Welcome broken Warrior to this
    House of Healing.
You have trudged through battlefields
on bones waiting to break
and finally be done with it.
But you stand before us tall and strong
    as you are sung about by bards.
There were battles won and battles lost and
    every one of them found you
    in the aftermath, defeated, wounded
    but alive and ready to push on
    to the next.
You've walked away from these so many times.
Your heart took the brunt of the attacks.
But we see a victor before us.
We don't see the wins and losses;
    we see you, here,
    seeking help for your
many collected wounds.

Stand firm on those capable bones and be
        proud of them.
We will show you how
        with the sonnets sung of you.
In this House, it is your strength
        we use to heal,
        and so shall you.

Welcome lost soul to this
        House of Hope.
There have been the darkest nights and blistering days
        and all have forced your eyes to your feet.
Terrains were rocky and steep and the miles
        were lost in eternity like apathy,
        like tree branches fallen without
        explanation;
        like rocks trying desperately for
        centuries to escape the mountain.
It feels like they would have nowhere to go.
You have rested beneath their instability, commiserating,
        worrying they would become lost.
You are not lost, but wandering.
You have left your mountain without a map
        and every destination along the way
        you found only yourself.
Tell us all your tales so that we might experience
        them with you.
Know with every word, you fill this
        House with hope.

Welcome Friend to this
House of Love.
We see you on your knees, weeping over
your broken heart –
it is full of scars and memories
you neither want,
nor want to lose.
It bathes in your tears and beats to the
rhythm of your wailing.
Let us hold it with you.
Let us add our tears to yours.
Let us harmonize our sobs and
be gentle with it
together.
And when our tears have run dry,
throats full of acorns,
Let us place it gently, with reverence,
amongst your greatest treasures.
We will be glad that you gave such a gift of love to
this House.

And we end this day,
Not weary, nor broken,
not lost nor alone, but
In Gratitude.

This house was built on the gifts of its guests.
This house is Rest.
This house is Healing.
This house is Hope.
This house is Love.
This house is your house.

You belong here.

This house is Poetry.

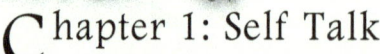

Chapter 1: Self Talk

This section is about the calming validation of speaking to yourself from a place of wisdom and self love. Poetry gives us the magic to find the healing words we need. Speak to your inner child with love and validation. Let your spirit become a conduit to channel messages from the Universe to your personality. As you read the following words, imagine it is your own inner Wisdom speaking to you. This is your initiation into practicing Poetry Magic: The Voice of Healing. Welcome, and thank you for your contribution to healing the world.

Let Us Be

Let us loft along this easy day, dear friend,
knowing all is always as it should be.

Let us seek proof in unwarranted smiles
   and whispers from
   the down of angels;
   from the danger
   and tranquility of broken ice;
   from the passing by of
   unmet acquaintances.
Let us let it lift us up,
   as if the blue above the mists
   were never hid, because
   we remembered clearly that
   in ancient times
   we chose
   the feeling of the earth
   between our toes
   knowing we were meant to soar.

9

Let us rest when we have counted all the stars
and polished each one with
the same care we give
to wished-for lilies.
They are seed pods of dreams
waiting for their turn to germinate;
waiting for us to walk on the soft earth;
waiting for us to repeat each
reason we have to love.
Let us giggle at dusk, calling forth
the growth of shadows:
they practice
their dance away from
the bright sun because they
are too bashful;
we shall be their guides.
Let us take off our shoes and our socks
and soak our bare feet in the
splendid truths
we've kept to ourselves
since we were old enough to
lose sight of invisible friends.
And while we're there, let us resurrect
them. They made us
gods; we can give them life.
Let us bathe our senses in the aftermath of rain
and wonder at how clean
the wash-water can become
since rinsing away internal narratives;
our stories need not be
of days past; they can
be epics of this easy day.

Let us let the day be day,
while we just
be.

As a Poet...
As a Man

As a man, I am fragile. Flesh and blood and fear of not paying bills. I need gas in the car when payday is still a week away and I still need food for my body.

I have breakable bones and a nine-to-five that inspires nothing but stress and doom. I sometimes fear
dying having accomplished nothing.

I listen to the words that escape my throat daily and find no solace in them. I wish away each painful day silently in my skull, and the wishes echo like a shrill gong.

As a poet, I am as fierce as a blazing dawn,
spreading passion across the horizon,
burning away the darkness;
the awe contained in dark thunderheads.
My lines are blinding bolts of raw energy:
threatening,
jagged and
beautiful.
The shapes of my words are etched patterns
on the smooth surfaces of the mundane,
illuminating the unseen
until it is unavoidable.
You can feel my poecy in your gut
and it tightens around your chest,
making it impossible to breathe.
But you wouldn't want to breathe for
fear of somehow lessening intensity.
I am a god of a Universe imagined,
immortal and unknowable.

As a man, I am awkward and shy. My human words bounce around, sometimes clever, sometimes witty, but usually, just… like… words people hear.

As a man I stand

always on the edges looking in, wondering what life must be like for everyone else, what place would I have among them, why can't they see me? Why can't they hear my words? Why can't I hear my words.

Why can't I speak my words?

Because... I am just a man.

As a poet, I am the epitome of passion.
I am glistening sweat beads on the flesh of lovers.
I am the hot breath of long sighs
released through lips when held breaths demand
escape.

I can conjure anticipation with my fingertips and
*   gently brush your cheek,*
*   trace your ear,*
*   run my fingers down your neck to your collarbone,*
The lust in my eyes makes you embrace your carnal cravings,
I draw gentle swirls around your shoulder,
*   painting portraits of desire on your flesh,*
*   and our lips and tongues connect*
I tickle the edges of your underarm before
*   tracing the roundness of your breast in*
*   circles growing smaller until*
I join my hands with lips and teeth and tongue and, as a poet,
I know just the places to kiss, to nibble... and bite... until
*   gooseflesh forms on your stomach,*
My fingers and hands remain, lightly pinching... massaging, but
my tongue deftly traces down,
*   down to your navel,*
*   circling your belly button for just a bit too long,*
*   biting, kissing, then down –*
*   you bite your lip through sweaty panic and anticipation –*
down a bit more until my hot breath touches you ...
*   "There," you say, "Oh please, right there" –*
you wiggle,
*   pressing your fingernails against my scalp*
*   resisting the urge to threaten me –*
I move closer, breath is hot you feel my lips, and...

As a man, I am a bumbling idiot. My insecurities shroud my visage with blandness and sadness, never giving me permission to speak anything but pleasantries to her. I, um, I can sometimes stammer and say really dumb things like, "Wanna see me put a cigarette out on my tongue?"

I run face first into a wall of ego – one of the walls that line my prison – blocking me from the sunlight of free verse.

But as a poet, I am the apex confidence.
I am a warrior poet: brandishing tempered steel words,
keen edged and even the spaces
between them are forged with meaning.
I slay my enemies effortlessly.
I dance the blade with grace and skill;
demand respect with: iron gaze, calm intent, steady
hands and
well-placed stance.

I turn a phrase over to reveal its soft underbelly.
I ride in with dawn and
race the sun to the opposite horizon.
I wake giants with laughter.
I rush the hordes, the dogs of war, the frenzied mobs and
mow them down with sharpened verse
and stand atop the field of battle bellowing my war cry,
I summon the gods of war to bow before my stanzas.

But as a man, I am unsure. I have far fewer answers than questions. Where do I fit? Who am I? Who am I today? How did I get here? What if I forget my lines? What if I cannot write anymore? I worry about you, about me... about us.

What if I don't wake up tomorrow?
Oh God, what if I do?

As a poet, I am the Universe.
Rumi speaks the thousand words for love
through my throat.
Virgil and Dante quietly guide me through
the darkness of my imagination.

As a man, I am minute.
A speck, barely noticeable walking down a not-so-busy street.

As a poet, I am a prophet.
I see meaning in everything, never definition.

As a man, I am a realist.
Everything must be explained.

As a poet, I am immortal.
As a man, I am frail, temporal.
As a poet, I am infinite.
As a man infinitely limited.
As a poet, lovable.
As a man, fallible.
A poet, enlightened.
A man, depressed.
A poet, free.
A man…
As a simple man…

As nothing more than
  just a man,

I am a poet.

Reflected

I have come to know you well,
though you have only glimpsed me.
I saw you when you weren't looking and it is clear to me
that you are so much more than you realize.
I have witnessed your doubt...
I have seen you falter...
I have seen inside you,
exposed to an inferno of your core –
where you were constructed most densely –
and there... before my vision swept... infinite Universes...

You were the stars
and the spaces in between.
You were slow swirling circles
of pinwheel galaxies illuminating
empty spaces of infinity. You were the brilliance
in a single electron excited along a piano's string:
it wept concertos by orchestras of stardust and
seduced mystical nebulae that drifted along waves
of space
and
time.

9

I stood in awe of who you were, knowing
you saw only your shadow laid carefully and precisely
on tall shafts of wild meadow grasses.

One day I saw you sipping tea beneath a bright full moon and

darkly clear skies dotted with everything knowable
between minute spaces of everything undiscovered.
You closed your eyes and didn't swallow as
upturned corners of your mouth arched in humble
thanksgiving;
you did not know that you were the flavor and
the tea was just tea.

One day I saw you watch a ladybug
tickle fine hairs on your arm and I heard you make a wish,
I saw joy sculpted in the lines of your face and it startled me.

I wished you could see that
you were answered prayers of a small one
desperate for a place to land –
a safe place –
but... my voice caught...
and my throat became unwilling to disturb ladybug prayers.

10

One day I heard you sing softly to yourself.
Your voice was barely a whisper;
little more than aspirated breath.
You were too shy...
and wanted no one else to hear,
but we did.
It became a love spell cast on all of Creation,
which prostrated at your feet sobbing seas of joy.
A chorus of wind harmonized and
meandering tufts of clouds played rainbow harps.
Infinity became an opera and,
unworthy,
I felt ashamed for listening,
for wishing you could hear it too.

One day I watched you stop to touch
the petals of a spring bud and
it sprang to life,
reaching up to feel your skin with silky petals;
your touch was love embodied.
Then you became the rain and the sunshine
and then you became
Life itself
and reaching for embrace,
the petals opened to reveal an entire universe you created.
And while life showered from your fingertips,
fields of wildflowers laughed and wept and danced with
playful, whirling breezes,
whispering poetry written by ancient, dainty, neutron stars
that played beyond the farthest reaches.
And you stood, leaning over a sweet new flower smiling.
Joy embraced your smile and you said, "Thank you!"
– as if the gift of love you gave was only yours received.
I saw a tear streak slowly down your cheek and
I broke.
Pieces of me fell to earth and broke again.
and again...
and again until my parts were less than dust motes
lighter than air – too light to fall.

So I floated
filled with something like sadness and ecstasy.
And I became separated from myself,
stretching out beyond edges of wildflower fields,
beyond rich earthy forests,
beyond frowning horizons.

I tried to tell you then – at that moment – what I saw,
but you could not hear my words.
They drifted past your ears as
something less than a gentle spring breeze –
something audible, but inarticulate.
You should listen carefully to quiet winds,
for they will sing to you secrets of who you are,
using lyrics you wrote yourself.

I know you sometimes wonder what you're worth.
I pray that you could see yourself as I do...
and I wonder what shapes known constellations would take if
you did.

You see, I need those gifts that only you have to share.
So, please, don't walk this day in doubt and fear.
And be aware, wherever in this Universe you wish that you
could go,
you should know,
I have already seen you there.

Sweet Soul

You've been fighting for so long, Sweet Soul –
bearing burdens bound tightly by fear and hurt,
on sagging shoulders, on
drooping hope.

You're tired and...
it's far too easy for the world to see.

But don't back down.
Not yet...
don't waver; don't hesitate.
press on, because despite the looming beasts ahead,
you are a warrior.

I know your struggle well,
though you hide behind a genuine smile,
the tired in your eyes reveal:

You feel everyone, Sweet Soul –
it shows in the worry stuck like sap on your brow,
in desperation tucked beneath your encouragement of everyone else,
in the tears that bleed from your soul, from your third eye...
you taste their fear,
you breathe their worries,
you vomit their hatred.
You become the lack of confidence cloaking those beautiful souls –
they deny possibility and embrace doubt like
cluttered debris stored too long in dusty corners of dark closets.
You become the lost happiness stuffed away by their judgments.
You become all the moments they did not risk it all for love,
their wasted minutes,
counted hours watching water boil,
days blotted out by extreme silence...

Try to remember, Sweet Soul –
        though it seems folded in your cortex –
none of it belongs to you!

You smile at a million blank faces every day
and even though busy smirks greet you back,
                keep
                        smiling!
Give them like gifts of crumpled flowers from a child.
Smile when blank faces return apathy.
Smile when confused scowls force-feed mistrust.

But stop!

Don't do it for them, Sweet Soul, but for yourself.
You smile because it's what you want the world to feel.
You love the undeserving because
you know the stuff on the surface
only veils the beauty beneath.
You hold them close to your heart because
you see what no one else sees.

Keep holding onto them, Sweet Soul,
because you know the truth…
that they deserve more than they believe,
that even though they fill you with their dread,
you get to swim in the hidden pools of their potential,
even if only for a lap or two.

You, Sweet Soul, have been led to this task.
You feel the strength in your veins,
surging through your strong shoulders,
your patient breath,
and your devotion to your warrior's task.

Don't give up.
Keep fighting.
Keep smiling.
Keep loving.

When Did You Forget...

When did you forget
        you are a Warrior?

        And... how?

Was it when your shoulders first slumped
        from need of rest?
Were you just too tired
        to notice the way
you rise like steam
under a cold winter sun
with an effortlessness
enviable by the hidden
deep of slow moving rivers?
You were the strength of rebellious mists
        no longer content in the security of
        the surface tension of waters.

You needed something more:
to soar with clouds
        that greet the moon:
        you were the one who reminded her
that the sun doesn't fall
when it sets.
You broke free –
        intentionally –
        with passion, and purpose,
        and a weathered smile on your face;
        it held the same defiance
        as the river's bed:

15

perhaps the water cuts away with time,
   but the earth beneath the deep persists,
         adapts
            and
loves the river anyway.

When did you forget
    you are a Warrior?
And was the forgetting temporary?

Was it with the questioning of value;
    when the world seemed to think you were
    a weed?
    And so what if it did?
    The Universe placed itself inside you when you
    were still a seed,
    and it waited there for
    Sunrise:
        there was always going to be a sunrise!

Did you also forget the
practiced strength of your patience?
    Or the tenacious blaze in your passions?
    Or the honed edges of your kindness?
    Or the solid steel of your determination?
    Or the way you love
the world anyway?

When did you forget
you are a Warrior?
How?

The Universe Will Breathe Once More

You were seeking the solace of the corner,
  living between breaths
  lips parted as if seeking words –
    wishing for words –
  wishing for a way to escape
  that feeling of heaviness in your chest.
Your eyes, downcast, searching the floor for
  skeletons of explanations.
The bones were bleached unapologetically white:
  like the failures of a blank page of poetry;
  like the jagged bite of fresh snow in five degrees –
    It steals all your senses, but pain.
Inhale

You did not   see me watching.
I tried to think of all the words I could that might
  fill the void the floor created
  and I whispered them to you:
    "You are enough"
I could not tell if you heard
    "You are strong"
But you had no reaction,
    searching for skeletons
    discovering sorrow instead
    "You are loved"
I saw your tears flooding like doubt
and I wanted to scream, just
to know if I had a voice at all...

Exhale

You have lived a warriors life; you've died a million times and
  reborn into a grander version and you've never
  lost your ability to love ferociously to insecurity. You
have survived
every fatal wound life inflicted and you carried torment

like adornments of gold,
not scars, not inadequacies, not bitterness.
Your wounds have always transformed into your hopes,
because you are a master of Love and these will too,
These will too.

Inhale

I know that you are worn and ragged.
And that you turn from me in times of need,
      but you always return when the
      breath you just took is finished.
My wish for you is that you spend less time
      between exhale and inhale, so that you might see
      the love I have for you.
      know that the love you fill the void with
      is what I am made of, and there is
        more than enough
      for you.
You deserve all the love:
      all there is to have;
      all there is to give.

Exhale

There is no space between night and day –
      no escape between breaths –
      no needs unmet when you reunite
        with your most precious jewel –
      and I wait impatiently for you to find
      that treasure sitting on the floor trying
      to hide, but glitters too brightly to remain
unnoticed.
You will see that precious jewel,
      I have no doubt.
And you will be surprised,
      like you have a thousand times before.
And you will embrace it and smile,
And the Universe will breathe once more.

You are not the Butterfly

You are not the butterfly.
You are the change that exists
between larva, pupa and flying free –
untethered by yesterday,
by unnecessary worries,
by fears of rejection...

You cannot be rejected because
you are worthy...
of everything worthy of you

Cast aside misconceptions of definitions of desire
and place, instead,
the lists of things your
heart demands. Place in all the empty spaces
of your...
          self...
all the wishes you deserve –
and you deserve them all –
to come true.

          Redefine a wish as an intuited gift,
          because those who would give it to you
          wait for you to ask.

You are not the butterfly.
You are not the chrysalis.
You are everything between, before and
after.
Transformations are most beautiful from
the inside, like
smiles are most beautiful at the exact moment
you feel the muscles
in your face engage, just before any
visible change takes place.

          That joy belongs to you

19

You have reason to smile.
You have reason to be happy.
You have reason to be sad.
And you have reason to allow it all to be
okay.
Because, you are okay.

You are not the butterfly.
You are not the caterpillar.
You are the Universe expressing itself
in its truest form of Love.
You are Love.
You have danced with Creation, sung duets
with Infinity...
You have wrestled with gods and celebrated
victories with Time.

You are not the butterfly;
You are the joy of the butterfly's wing.
You are the awe found in color and line
delighting in summer's warmth under cloudless skies
as the slow swinging wing soaks up sunrays to dry
this new found freedom that has been
painted to perfection, and

you are that perfection;

you are the careful attention paid by the expanse of the Universe
to make such a wing become perfection;

You are more than just an idea;
more than a simple metaphor;
more than someone who has changed;
you are more than the butterfly...

Discussion: Self Talk

My early life gave me more reasons to doubt, and even despise myself as an adult. As a child, I was instilled with the belief by an abusive step-father that I was worthless. As an adult, his voice became my inner voice. It seemed easier to believe I had no value so that when people validated that belief, it wouldn't hurt as bad.

Creating New Internal Voices

Life, therapy, and medication have helped me to cope with those voices. Poetry Magic taught me to create new voices. I add them to the choir. It has given me the power to have compassion for those negative voices. It has taught me that I am not entirely powerless over my past and that healing is attainable. Poetry Magic can tame the inner demons, quiet their voices, expose their pain, and even surround the spaces they occupy with love and compassion.

In chapter 5, we will talk about using Poetry Magic to learn to love. Self talk is the foundation of Love. It is through self talk that we begin to learn to love ourselves.

Welcome to a New Perspective of Yourself

Poetry Magic can (and **will!**) help you see yourself with new vision. Poetry Magic *wants* you to feel valued, worthy of love, special and important.

We are talking about self worth. From the same, familiar perspective we've always used, we are powerless to change our measure of our own worth. But to cast a poem using Poetry Magic, it requires you to change the perspective you use to obtain that measure.

Borrowing Someone Else's Perspective

I wrote the poem "Reflected" during a time when I

was desperate to feel valued. People around me consistently demonstrated their love for me, but my internal narrative was too loud to hear anything else. At the time, I was reading a lot of Rumi. One night, while I was feeling ready to try something different to cope with my depression, I wrote "Reflected."

I let the Universe speak to me through Rumi's voice. And I let the magic weave the lines that became the first draft of "Reflected." This poem has been an amazing tool for me to help myself and others heal. I have wept at it. I have seen others weep at it.

Please, go read "Reflected" (pg.10) *out loud*. As you read it, imagine the Universe is speaking to you using your mouth. Listen to your voice.

Go, now... go do that right now. I'll wait right here...

Practice
Now it's your turn.

1) You are going to Summon powerful and loving entities to cast your magic. Think of someone or something that embodies the idea of Love to you. Maybe a family member. A character in a movie. Maybe it's an angel, or other mystical being. Maybe it's your dog or your cat.
2) Now in your mind imbue them with the infinite wisdom of the Universe. You have now called forth the most powerful being in existence. This entity has manifested for you as an entity that loves you. Hold on to this entity for a few minutes.
3) When you're ready, start writing your poem and allow this entity to speak a message you need to hear from it.
4) Now share it! Write it in the spaces on the next few pages.

Chapter 2: Giving Space to Pain

What seems broken and cannot be fixed is, in fact, perfect and whole as it is. Poetry can paint portraits of our broken parts, and express the fears, doubts, and traumas that we keep buried. Healing means allowing these parts of us to share our daylight. It means to get to the brightness of the light, we must journey through to release them. This is an act of Self-love.

Some of the following poems seem dark. Some may be triggering and will talk about things like: suicidality, mental illness, body dysmorphia, and so on. The magic these have brought to my life is unparalleled. And the healing effects of their magic have spread to others.

Shine your magic poetry light in the corners of your psyche and be alone never more.

Dysmorphia

Dysmorphic reflections filter in: Fear, Sadness and Waning Hope.
Love is filtered out completely... replaced by
                        wishes and laughing fantasies.
Confidence is filtered out completely... replaced by
                        unreachable fitness goals.
On a scale, gravity is honest,
but through these reflections, gravity is cruel and not constant;
a body can become dense and massive.
Beauty is scratched off surfaces, revealing cracks and bumps and popping veins, the relentless, jagged-tooth gnawing of time, and bulbous blemishes.

That which is reflected in perfect mirrors can no longer be seen.
That which looks at this broken mirror
will no longer see that which is looking,
It will only witness what is seen.
But it cannot be seen,
because this dysmorphic reflection never displays truth.
It flatters and condemns.
Accuracies are bent by moody opinions.
Yet always… that which looks, desires to see the truth,
but how?
How!

How!
But how?
Yet always… that which looks, desires to see the truth.
Accuracies are bent by moody opinions.
It flatters and condemns.
because this dysmorphic reflection never displays truth.
But it cannot be seen,
It will only witness what is seen.
will no longer see that which is looking,
That which looks at this broken mirror
That which is reflected in perfect mirrors can no longer be seen.

Dysmorphia flashes across *the face of a mirror:*
disfigured, bloated and alien.
It is other.
Other than that to which it belongs.
It is a reflection of something beautiful,
but the reflection is not.
It is hideous.
It is broken flesh.
It is worn and stretched:
scarred with a thousand years of inadequate attention.
It has become too many shades of red.
It penetrates reality with fictions,
with its own horrors
with its own fractured spaces.
It drips.
It mucks in puddles on dirty floors.
It clots.

It clogs, damming stale pools of disgust.

The reflection does not reflect what resides behind the broken flesh!
It cannot reflect the beating heart that pushes lifeblood through this body.
It cannot reflect the strength stored in vast pools of potential.
This lens should never be used as a tool for evaluation.
No!
The unreflected body can only truthfully be seen through the eyes of a lover.
The eyes of a lover do not see dysmorphic reflections.
Suffice it to say – to see the truth –
the looker must come to love what it cannot see with looker's eyes...

The looker must become the lover.
The looker must become the lover.

I want to become the lover!
I want to hear the kindness in the poetry that flows from my hands.
I want to remove the safety and sadness of my mistrust.
I want to wrestle the strength life has built on my capable shoulders.
I want to swim in the vast pools of my potential, all of my potentials.

I can hear the lifeblood pumping in my inner ear,
and each beat of my heart fills my body with passion
and when I begin to overflow with each new joy,
I let it shower outward through these lines I love.
I bend and sway in lyric winds with more love than
surface reflections contain,
and I want to give it all to you.

I want to capture beauty on a page and paint the world.
I want to laugh among the serious crowds of worker
bees.
I want to sing to giant mountains waiting for something
to dance to.
I want to play hide and seek with old forests.
I want to splash playfully into the old stories of passing
babbling brooks.
I want to shed my clothes and inhibitions and climb the
tallest tree to let the sun touch my skin and radiate
beauty.
Just be beautiful.

This is what I want to see when I look in the mirror,
but it doesn't exist on the surface,
No! I have to go outside to look inside...
I have to look inside to see the outside.

All I Am...

Sometimes, all I am is broken bones –
glued into a rickety framework of antiquated identities.
I must be brittle, breakable by the breath of a simple change
in voice.
I must be dry, waiting to fall to dust
and become a pile in a shadowed corner:
safe from winds of change that seek
to scatter me to indistinction.

Sometimes, all I am is a whisper.
lost in the din of conversations;
as visible as a breath behind forced laughter...
I must be the frightened thought no one was supposed to hear,
uttered but rescinded on the next nervous inhale:
never again repeated,
but quietly echoed within the confines
of a worried mind.

Sometimes, all I am is wishes.
Carried on glowing tails of meteors
who refuse gifts of weightlessness
for a single chance to light up the darkness,
I must ride a very thin tail of hope
that I will not burn up in atmosphere.
I must be the last lit candle on a birthday cake:
Everyone sees me, but no one wants to be the one to say,
"you had to get them all to get your wish..."

Sometimes, all I am is an autumn seed in spring --
a dream remembered
among the oddities of new life...
I must be too deeply rooted in expectations of winter...
I fear the wind that wants to dance with me,
that desires to carry me to places containing
the fertile space I need to grow.

Sometimes, all I am is trapped inside my head.
And it is frustrating.
I can see my mind in the distance, and I
appear to be afraid…
I want to expect the worst and allude it
or risk being blown away into oblivion...
I want to stay in the void that isolates me
from the danger of atmosphere.
I wish I knew how to paint
new visions of safety and confidence.
But…

Sometimes, I can change my perspective
and the Universe becomes a new place where
I am happy.
Sometimes, I become the infrastructure of a thriving life
that once seemed like a daydream.
Sometimes, I am the birth of my goals.
Sometimes, I am color and substance.
Sometimes, I am brave.
Sometimes, I am enough:
      just as I am…

I have made myself into a ghost of flesh,
stretched taught across my many incarnations.
While I lay dying under the worried gaze of Venus —
as I searched for any small thing to love —
I vomited my very last seed of Hope.
It fell from my throat, between sobs,
feather-light and frothy,
burning through the snow and
onto the wanting ground.
It was the most beautiful green bile —
gentle, compassionate —
like foam, but the color of what I wish
were all the gifts of Spring...
It touched the ground sweetly;
in the way lovers dream of caressing each other
with practiced fluency.
And then it sunk into the lonely earth.

Beautiful

Green

Bile

Let me tell you about oxycodone:
When healing from shoulder surgery,
   5 milligrams will help you sleep at night.
Your mouth will be dry, like the brown paper sacks
      you used to carry home something sweet,
      something to smile about.
And when padded slings forbid
      habits of sleeping on your stomach,
      5 milligrams will help you fall asleep on your back.
5 milligrams will quiet nerves that manifest
      when she smiles and asks if there's anything you need.
5 milligrams will help you forget —
      just a little—
      that you feel more than self-conscious.
5 milligrams will make you forget to wonder if you snore...

I have become an expert in constructing custom prisons...
I build them with only one exit...
I become the warden and the guard...

31

I have already been the judge and jury...
And I reserve the only cell for myself.
I paint the walls with vivid memories of
*   nightmares lived long ago,*
*   when the souls   of helplessness and confusion*
*   were both only seven years old,*
*   and prisons were constructed with*
*   belt buckles and bare skin...*

10 Milligrams will knock you out!
After the first night post-op, it will teach you
        that five is all you need to fall asleep.
10 milligrams is the dose you take when
        you've never taken oxycodone before.
It will prove to you that your
        knowledge of narcotics is stored in your brain
        in the same place as fear, naiveté,
        and the wish that she is the one.
10 milligrams will help you forget to be embarrassed
        about the strangling white post-op tights
        you have to wear in front of her...
10 milligrams is not enough to put your wishes
        and desires to rest for a night –
        you'll still look into her eyes
        and dream of falling deeply in love...
at least, you'll dream until you fall asleep.

He was broken, but he ate fish anyway.
A gift of sympathy or apology,
*   he swallowed and it tasted like emptiness*
*   and confusion.*
Nine years old and bleeding his need for Love...
It spilled down the backs of his legs from
*   his broken flesh*
*   and shattered heart.*
It pooled around his ankles, and rose to his
*   knees, his chest, his head...*
*   it choked his skill at loving freely...*
Nine years old and he was told,

"Love is earned but you will never be able to afford it!"
He was broken, but
> *he did not go to bed hungry...*

80 milligrams will send you to the emergency room,
> according to Google searches.

80 milligrams is not a destination,
> it is where your plan begins,
> the trail-head of you very last hike.

80 milligrams won't set her worried mind at ease —
> or is it her hopeful mind?

80 milligrams won't decrease her stress or stop
> her rage.

It certainly won't meet her demands.
It won't make her happy.
80 milligrams won't make you rich enough for her...
> but that life insurance might.

80 milligrams certainly won't glue
> your dolorous heart back together.

80 milligrams is not enough,
> just like you are not enough...

80 milligrams won't kill you;
> it is a call for help.

But you don't want to call for help any more...

He has loved...
He has loved his lovers.
He has loved every pet he's ever had, and
> *every pet he's been introduced to.*

He's loved his friends, his family, his neighbors,
> *lonely transients looking for spare change...*

He has loved the mountain air,
> *the cold rain,*
> *and even sharp winters.*

Hell, he's even loved you...
But he never knew how to love himself enough
> *to battle his way out of*
> *memories of abuse that replayed*
> *in his mind and in his life.*

He's spent his whole life choking on his
inner child's blood.

120 milligrams should do the trick.
120 milligrams is 24 five-milligram pills.
120 milligrams does not roll easily in your hand;
        you have to push them around with your finger
        if you want to see them move.
120 milligrams looks so harmless –
        24 small white pills look more like
        doubt than fear.
120 milligrams is the amount you hold on your
        shaking palm just before
        you pray to the Universe for an alternative.
They go down so easily.
120 milligrams tastes a little like surprise,
        a little like relief...

I'm so sorry that I hurt you.
That was not my intent.
I wanted her to know what it felt like to be loved.
I saw into her soul.
Maybe I shouldn't have looked, but
        I couldn't help myself.
The way she looked at me drew me in
        and her eyes became heroin to me.
I mistook that look for Love,
        but it was hunger.
I let her wear my heart around her neck.
And later, I saw her pain;
        it looked a lot like mine.
I was still learning how to love mine,
        but when we met,
        I tried to love hers instead.
I wanted to hold her and prove to her that
        she deserved the Universe,
        that,

if one of us made it through this
life alive,
maybe we'd both be ok someday.
But... I wasn't enough,
and that wasn't what she wanted from me.
I see that now.
I saw it too late.
For what little it's worth –
I loved her more than life itself.
She loved a clause in my policy.
I'm sorry...

315 milligrams is a final escape.
When the rest didn't open any doors,
315 milligrams must be the skeleton key.
315 milligrams dot the darkness like midnight stars
through a thin haze that grows too thick too fast.
They echo through the canyon like sobs that
only the most forlorn could ever hear.
315 milligrams will taunt you for 26 hours
when you are alone in the forest.
It wakes you up every two hours,
holding your breath in front of your face
like your step-dad held his belt —
like the way she held her smile when she said,
"Hell yes, I'd kill you for a million dollars." —
both of them wearing looks of joy and rage.
315 milligrams will cause you pain,
like your step-dad wielded his belt —
like she wielded words like poisoned daggers —
with something more than enthusiasm.
315 milligrams is enough to kill all of the Love.

But no amount of oxycodone will be enough when
the Universe freely gives you
the alternative you prayed for.
It's not enough to hide the fact that
you have always been your alternative.
It's not enough to keep you from ending

35

*the living memories abuse you've
carried within you for so long.
It's not enough to keep you from being
remade when you have died.
Now, it's time to let yourself be loved –
there are so many who have been trying
and so many more that will try,
let them...
And now it's time to love yourself –
as much as you have tried to love
everything
else.*

Flames and Fire

Flames and fire,
comfort's wish, but the brushing of hands...

a shoulder: clothed but bare and empty
the world spins and turns within
and a broken brain becomes a body
        trapping reels on replay
        simple mistakes that take
        days and weeks of history:
        a flame and a fire
colorful bins, empty
        an overcooked egg
        dogshit and dogfood and
piles of clean laundry
broken bedframes
eons of old ice covered sidewalks
a dresser with three drawers
a cast iron frying pan burning like dead wood
a flame and a fire and the brushing of hands
the wish for comfort burned
by the brushing of hands
hands brushing
        brushing away
        brushing
        rejecting
        brushing
        rejecting
and the world spins and turns within and...
though no one dies today,
        the lights inside turn dim
and silence sobs on railroad tracks

                    waiting...

I May Be Cracked...

I may be cracked, but I am unbroken.
The lines ahead of you were etched into a lifetime;
    they evoke a brilliance in the shadow of hindsight.
These lines follow no predictable pattern –
    no shape of
           familiarity.
They are fault lines,
        interrupting memories like
   earthquakes and blame
       like
         wisdom and shame.
You can see the landscape of my recollections ripped apart by
   friends that were not friends at all.
These lines split my trust in two.
They played with my mind like a hacky sack,
   performing feats with their feet
     as they kicked me right in the trust.

This landscape was fractured by a girl with
   a smile that spread from her mouth to her eyes
    to my ability to focus on life --
      she played with my heart like a yoyo,
      like a champion until
        the string broke and
          I stopped returning every time.
           Easily replaceable.
And another girl I wanted desperately to love, but she only
wanted to play with my…
And another, who desperately wanted to love me, but I only
wanted to play with her….

If you examine these cracks, my soul will spill
   from them
   and I won't be able to stop the tidal flood.

I will leak and make a mess and be reduced to
a puddle of something that was there
before the cracks were made.
I will have to collect myself with dirty rags
woven of something like poetry.
I will sweep myself into a pile with my pen.
I will collect myself with words and incantations.

And I cannot miss a single piece,
because when pieces fall away,
I have to glue them back to fill
the empty
spaces,
because this is what I am,
and I have to retain my shape,
or lose   my   form.

I am the ugly mug in the cupboard.

I may be cracked, but I'm not broken.
I might be soft, but I'm not weak.
I am calloused where others are too sensitive.
I stand tall in the face of dangers:
Like success...
Like meeting new people...
Like seeing a baby beaver swim in the creek in my
back yard
and having no one to tell about it...
Like remembering that time I made it
to the top of a new mountain with
no witness with which to reminisce...

My strength is painted with
compassion and concern –
with an overwhelming desire   that
YOU will always have someone
to witness you.

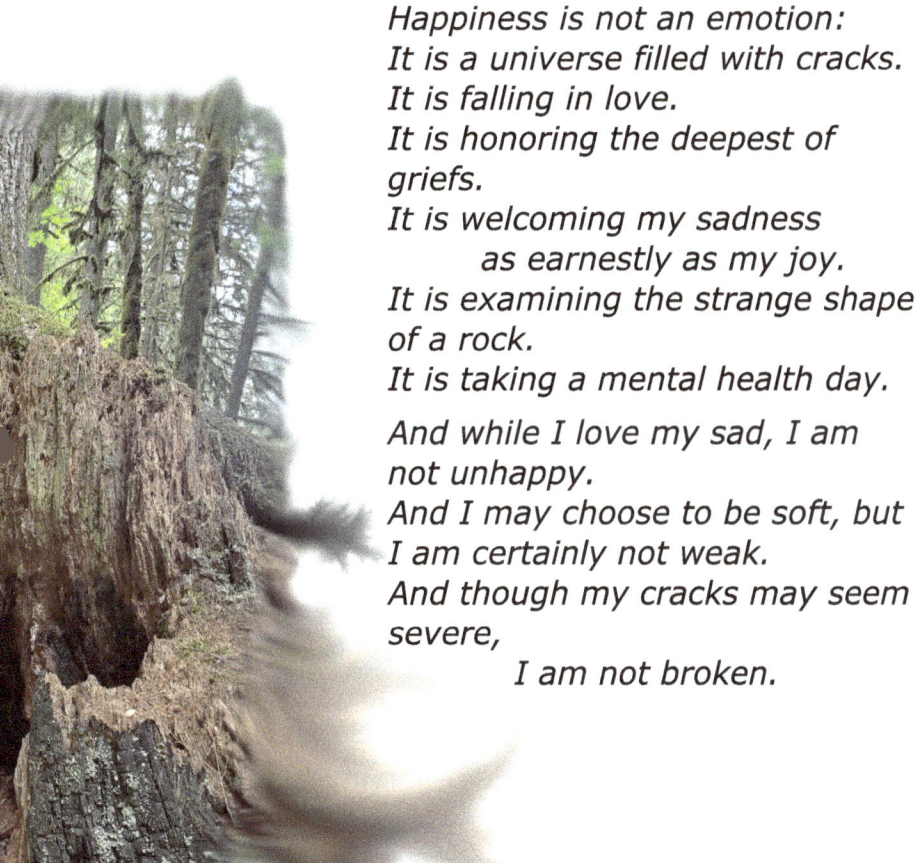

I may be cracked, but I'm not broken.
I might be soft, but I'm not weak.
I might get sad, but I'm not unhappy.

I vow to no longer deny what happens inside --
or disguise it with a fake smile wrapped
in fears of rejection.

Happiness is not an emotion:
It is a universe filled with cracks.
It is falling in love.
It is honoring the deepest of
griefs.
It is welcoming my sadness
as earnestly as my joy.
It is examining the strange shape
of a rock.
It is taking a mental health day.

And while I love my sad, I am
not unhappy.
And I may choose to be soft, but
I am certainly not weak.
And though my cracks may seem
severe,
I am not broken.

Words
of
Ghosts

The words of ghosts are hard to hear.
        when they bite the parts of me that
        want for better times and
        wish for the swift end of this
absolute darkness.

Though her mouth is distant and closed
        I can hear her speak.
        I can see her tongue
                coated with bitterness, and
                to me it looks too much like suffering.
I would feed her love.

I want to understand her words, though
        they remain incoherent and trace
        misunderstanding with a thick, black,
        impenetrable stroke.
these her walls.

I cannot breach these walls when my own voice
        is carried into the thickness of the forest
        on the thickness of the fog that
        threatens our eternity.

This pain feels deeper to me than her memory.
This wound is below our skin,
        on the surface of our muscles,
        making it impossible to move.
These thoughts feed from corpses of beasts
        that were never slain, but
        also never lived.

I am the center of this silent chaos.
I am also the victim of this quiet.

This calm is cancerous.
This fear is air too cold to breathe.
These wants are hopeless and powerful
        beyond the wants of me,
        beyond the wants of right and good.
I am prey to this calm.
I am lost in this silence.

I feel myself fading from her memory,
        unslain and never having lived.
I want to fight, like a man trying not to drown,
        that she might know again,
the love I give can break this calm
and it kills me to know that this is what she fears.

But now I fear winning this fight, and feel
        I might be better off being swallowed by water.

The words of ghosts are hard to hear,
        when what they say is nothing,
        when history is divided in two.

The world is made to become unfamiliar,
                again,
        when the words of ghosts are silent.

She is my ghost.
        I am her history.
We are silence.
We are silence.

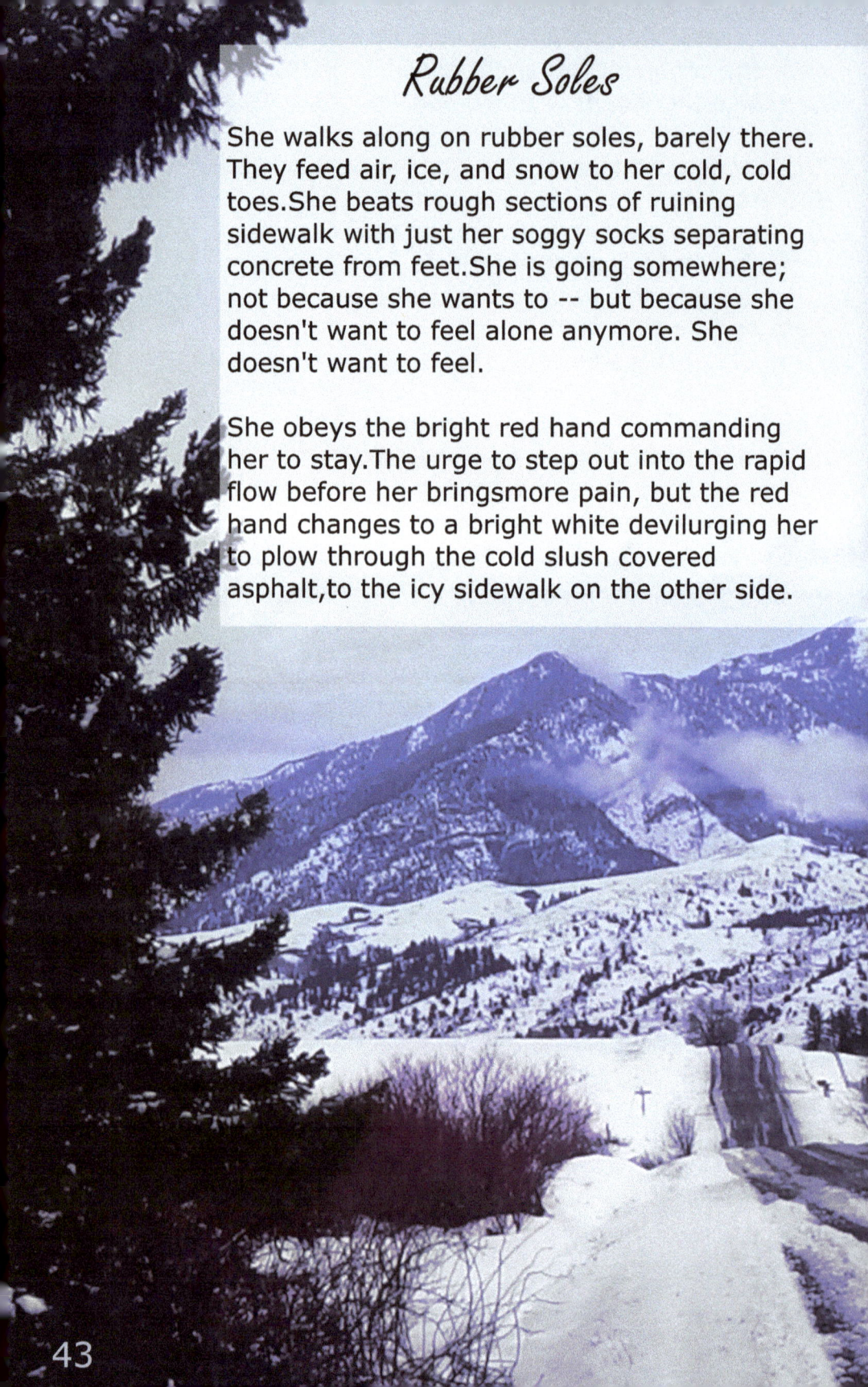

Rubber Soles

She walks along on rubber soles, barely there.
They feed air, ice, and snow to her cold, cold
toes.She beats rough sections of ruining
sidewalk with just her soggy socks separating
concrete from feet.She is going somewhere;
not because she wants to -- but because she
doesn't want to feel alone anymore. She
doesn't want to feel.

She obeys the bright red hand commanding
her to stay.The urge to step out into the rapid
flow before her bringsmore pain, but the red
hand changes to a bright white devilurging her
to plow through the cold slush covered
asphalt,to the icy sidewalk on the other side.

She swallows fear.

She doesn't think about the ground she feels through socks worn already three days in a row wet from sweat and snow.She does not think about new shoes... nor the good ol' dayswhen trips to a friend's house was made in the back seat of mom's car... nor the days when it always seemed to take so long for the bus to arrive... nor when a chocolate bar was aforbidden treat. She just wants not to be alone.

So she crosses the street, despite numb feet and broken soul and worn out rubber soles; despite knowing the hurt she'll cause too many people when they find her with a belly full of something someone at her destination will give her, or from something she smoked, something swallowed, something pushed into her veins.

She won't have known what it was.
She won't have noticed slipping away.
She will not feel anything, any more.

Little Bird

Alight yourself upon my shoulder, little bird,
and rest your broken wings.

You've been soaring
so far
for so long
between
blinded winds –
they have become too strong to lift you up –
and the dusty earth:
too dry and worn to hold you steady.

You were never meant for Limbo,
    but it's hosts have known
    joy for your visit,
    and sent prayers of hope for you
    when you found your way again
    and departed their company.

You have earned your place, here, in this world, little bird,
    by perching on
the mantle of the waking morning
    and searching for the loneliest sky;

The empty sky was made for you,
by the feathers of
your own weary wings,
and we have been watching you
paint perfection in the clouds,
grateful for your efforts,
saddened by your struggles.

45

The view where you have been has stretched
beyond feature in all directions,
and your eyes have been searching
for horizons that hold precious landmarks,
and I'm sorry your
eyes have become so dry and
your vision so blurred:
you have been waiting to blink, but
afraid if you do the Universe will
move beyond your view.

Fear not!
We will always wait for you.

You may rest now, little bird, and
close your eyes,
and though you may not see us,
        know
        you are not
        alone
        in this world.

We have been here all along, blowing
gentle breaths against the winds that
push against you
(you should know,
they never doubted your strength).

We have wept for feeling the aches you have endured
        and shed our tears to settle the
        dust of the dry Earth;
        she has mourned for simpler times
        when you could love the sky
        for being empty.

Don't mourn flightless lives, little bird,
        for your greatest moments
        lie in the fallen leaves
        of barren trees

46

that long for winter's end;
it comes – soon enough –
with the rising of the Pheonix sun.

And don't fear losing your voice from singing;
the moon opens her eyes
to shine her light
on the colors of your quiet song
so the stars might see who
they have been dancing to.
Sing until your heart stops
for joys that cannot be spoken,
but fill the stillness of time
between heartbeats.

We have daydreamed of you.

Your wings?
They have not been broken.

Your song?
It was never quiet
in the choir.

Your life?
it has always been
our most revered treasure:
every sacred moment of it

But rest here now, little bird,
and I will carry you –
for a time –
whispering jewels into your ears
until you remember
who made the sky
and who it was made for…

Discussion: Giving Space to Pain

It's instinctive – even hard-wired into the most primal parts of our brains – to avoid pain. The idea of giving it space seems... weird. But the thing is, pain exists. That part of you that is hurt is (instinctively) neglected. It very well may be that your pain will be with you for the rest of your life. But if you give it space and consequently, care, you welcome that part of your being back into the entity that is You. By giving your pain space, you can begin to heal it.

My Pain

Body dysmorphia is an issue that rears its ugly head (pun?) when I feel vulnerable about my appearance. Dating, performing on stage, or going to a party where I don't know anyone are examples of times that my body image is skewed beyond reality. I first recognized it when I went from weighing 265lbs to 160lbs in less than a year. I went to the gym for 2 hours every day, would trail run, hike, and turned every move I made into a way to exercise somehow.

On one hand, I was learning that the limits I had always believed I had were very heavily miscalculated. On the other hand, there was a very hurt part of me that believed I didn't deserve to be loved. It was easy to body shame myself internally when I was big, but not so easy when I was becoming happy with what I saw in the mirror. That hurt part of me had the power to change what I saw.

I remember one day, specifically, looking in the mirror and thinking that I was gaining weight again. I had plateaued at 165lbs at this time in my life. I was about to step on the scale, expecting 170lbs (maybe more). But the scale said 160lbs. I looked at my reflection then back to the scale. I stepped off, checked the zero on the scale (it was good), stepped back on: 160lbs. The mirror said otherwise. The same mirror I had been trusting all this time.

My therapist introduced me to the concept of body dysmorphia. After learning more and more, it was very clear that I could no longer trust what I saw in the mirror. Education and awareness did not get rid of it. In fact, I still experience body dysmorphia to this day. I probably always will. And that's actually ok, because I no longer use the mirror to judge myself (well, most of the time).

My dysmorphia stems from some deep childhood traumas that left me with a set of beliefs about myself that are core to me. It's easier for my monkey brain to assume I'm not worthy of Love, because I didn't feel worthy of Love as a child. If I don't try, I don't have to have the belief validated.

Using Poetry Magic to Give Space to Pain
I wrote the poem "Dysmorphia" as a way to give my self judgment space. You can see by the end of the poem, that *I took control of that judgment*. The tools our mind develops when we are not participants can be atrocious. When we choose to participate in developing and utilizing tools, we heal.

And that's why we give our pains the space they require. We expose them, and then we can see what loving tools we need to develop to help them begin healing.

49

Practice

Now you try!

*(**NOTE**: This can certainly be a very triggering practice. Please feel free to skip this practice for as long as you need. If you feel ready in the future to come back to it, know that you are not alone!)*

1) There is a belief you have about yourself you know is wrong. Think about the belief itself. Imagine it is separate from you. Put it in a bucket, or some other container, in front of you. It came from you, but in the bucket, it is not a part of you.

2) With your hands, mold the substance from the bucket into a statue, or mannequin or some other structure that has a mouth, but does not have any power of mobility. It can't hurt you. Also, it can only speak when you allow. You are in control, but it does have it's own thoughts and words.

3) Give it a voice and let it speak for as long as you choose.

4) When you're ready, use it's words to start a rough draft of a poem.

5) Your poem is not complete! Use your powers of self-talk from Chapter 1 to finish the poem! Speak to the part of you that the pain came from. Speak to the pain itself. Wash the pain with love and kindness.

6) When it is clean, take it back into you and let the light continue to shine on it in the space it occupies.

7) When you've looked at the poem you just cast, and are satisfied with the magic it is emanating, please write it in the spaces provided in the next few pages.

Chapter 3: Changing Perspective

From our current perspective, there are limited possible ways to perceive. We can't see through walls if a building is in the way, but we can change the possible perceptions available to us by walking around the building, changing our perspective.

Similarly, we cannot see through the pain when we are in it in order to heal when our perspective is blocked by the darkness of our trauma. Poetry Magic gives us the creative power to move around the pain, but first, we need to identify where our current perspective is emanating from.

When we're struggling from that darkness, we can use Poetry Magic to shine a light on it. These poems do just that. Since we've given space to our pain, we can now move around and let our poetry see things another way.

Plain Brick Walls

He awoke in the shadows cast against his plain brick walls:
no door, tall windows with a view of only the sky.
These cracked and crumbling bricks leaked mortar
like skin stained with old blood,
from old wounds that never healed –
wounds from battles neither lost nor won, but over now.
He could panic, but the walls had long ago become familiar.
Though the air was stale and the packed-dust floor too hard,
existing in futility defeated hope and want for freedom.
His soul had become stale and too hard.

This prison became a fortress.
The inescapable echoes of his breath became musical,
and at times, conversational.
He too was cracked and crumbling.

He stopped trying to remember how he came to be in this place.
He stopped trying to remember if there was life before.
There were vague memories he wasn't sure were his;
memories of falling in love,
of finding joy and art and life and breath...
but these visions seemed more like imagination than
recollection.

There was no world beyond these walls;
at least, none quite as interesting as
how this prison had become safety.

How long had he been there?
A question that crept into his thoughts from time to time,
but he laughed it away without smiling.
He had always been there.
It was all there was.

There were shadows, and light from cracks.
And when a sunbeam pushed through,
it sometimes landed on his face –
blinding him – and a voice inside would try to
use his mouth to scream.
Sometimes he would find himself reaching for the sun,
to touch the alien warmth that seemed to want to
burn away the damp darkness,
that wanted to germinate stray seeds of hope,
that wanted to set fire to the prison walls.

One day...
He touched a crack in the wall...
Pieces fell to the dirt floor,
raining red dust slowly –
the inevitable failed rebellion of façade –
and the thin beam of light grew brighter...
He looked out –
"out" tasted odd on his tongue –
dimly witnessing blurred colors below what must have been a horizon
and bright blues and wispy whites above.

"These are sky and life," he thought.
He dug more, confused as to what he was digging for.
Soon, the crack became a hole, and the blurred visions beyond
became scenes he could describe with all the words
he had not forgotten how to use,
and somewhere beyond his reasoning,
his fortress once again became a prison
and the outside became a holy land.

His words became metaphor once more.

The warmth of sunlight now shining brightly on his face
ignited his passion and rage and he became so wild with vigor
that he did not notice his tightly clenched fists,
nor his warrior's stance,
nor the roar pushing out from his deeply filled lungs through his
stretched lips.
He did not stop his fists from beating against the bricks,
until the hole became a chasm
and the walls began to tremble with each
forcefully   delivered   blow.
Soon enough the walls shook of their own volition,
as if the prison itself became engrossed with fear
and finally...
collapsed to rubble around him...

What was left was:
a pile of bricks and red dust
like old blood
that could no longer block the open air
and meadows filled with a life that had been living
the whole time
one he had always been a part of.

You and I...
we only think we're good at constructing prisons...
but our constructions always fall...

55

Oldering World

Somehow, the world grew up, though I do not know when. This morning, when I awoke, it was all so different and yesterday might have been the same. I'm not sure when it changed, but it was no longer young. It no longer bears new days on strong shoulders, but awakes each morning weary... tired. It no longer orbits the sun in a playful dance, twirling beneath brilliantly lit peep holes into infinite possibility. Some time before, it did these things and was sadly unaware that today would not be the same.

"I need some coffee," said the world to me, dark circles surrounding sad eyes, face drooping with wrinkles that were not there last night, "...and a smoke. Don't talk to me until after."

Somehow, the world grew up and I do not know how. It used to never sleep; it doesn't seem that long ago it held careless vigor in the palm of my hand. Troubles began hiding behind stuff that needed to get done – the sorts of stuff grown-up minds try to convince you are irresponsible if left undone. I'm pretty sure it didn't set out to grow up. Had it known this would happen, I'm thoroughly convinced it would have treasured each moment, loved more deeply, laughed harder... from deep in the gut.

"God... where in the hell did the day go," asked the world in bewildered frustration, squinting at the clock on the living room wall, dimly lit by the failing light of the autumn dusk through the window.

Somehow, the world grew up, but I cannot figure out why. I remember clearly, sometime ago, it brought joy to hope filled days, but now seems preoccupied trying to pay bills, when it is able. It worries about responsibilities and things it never would have before were they not dangerous like: self-pollution, defor-estation (and whether or not it was caused by wear-ing hats too much), and not missing the morning alarm.

"I don't know how I'm supposed to pay the utilities," the world muttered, barely audible through tight lips, head down in either humility or humiliation, nose pointing at a folded piece of paper, "They're just too high."

Somehow, I think I may grow up soon as well. But the condition that the world is in for doing so is not a very convincing argument. I think I'd rather remind it how to dance and laugh and love carelessly, again. I want to point out that grace periods are for grace, not worry. That time is spent, whether we enjoy it or not. That coffee is infinitely more than just caffeine. That bills don't go away now matter how much you pay, but neither do sunrises, sunsets, happy puppies, shared smiles, hugs, dandelions, mud and toes, mushrooms, grilled cheese and tomato soup, happi-ness...

We are not Big Yet

We are not big yet. But we are growing.
We have not filled in our feet
that want to walk, no,
        stomp across the Universe!
We want to know it all,
and plant our flag in every
orbiting rock we can find in the vast black skies above.
We want to create insight,
yet we are made by it.
Because we are not big yet.
We are little.
We are fragile.
We are still very small.

I've heard it said the energy released
by a hydrogen bomb is roughly equal to
the energy stored in the atoms of one kitten:
helpless... defenseless... lost – *like us* – in blind courage
and *entirely* unafraid!
Maybe we should to be more afraid?
No!
We play!
We tear across the comfort of living room carpets.
We walk on shaky legs, still unfamiliar with gravity
and look out into the Universe with eyes barely opened
where we see so much and want to touch it all,
to feel it with our paws.

I've heard it said one second of our sun is like a billion kittens.
One billion kittens brightly shining at the center
of orbiting bodies of ancient, sleeping gods
and we yearn to play with them,
                        to wake them up!

A billion kittens grow gardens and rain-forests and
sunburns on treeless beaches when we left the
                              sunscreen in the car,
too far away to bother with.
They do it with a gaze.
One billion kittens hissing,
trapped in layers of atmosphere
bouncing from stratosphere to troposphere
stopping at the tropopause to lick their paws
before growing hot with frustration,
arching backs and batting attacks with needle toes
at skin exposed to the unintended rage
of one billion kittens who define the shade,
while scratching cancers more and more as
days pass deeper into the
frayed, twisting ends of this story.

But their rage is not our fault...
because we are not big yet.
We are only now just learning to walk.
We hobble on shaky legs unaccustomed to gravity.
We open brand new eyes and look out
beyond the blueness of the skies we see
to the center of a galaxy we cannot quite reach.
And there we see a black hole exactly equal to
billions of billions of kittens
        stretching limbs...
              quietly feeding on stars...
lapping from the Milky Way oblivious to me and you.
To these billions of billions of kittens we are no threat!
And they pose no threat to us, yet they
  scratch small rips in the skin of
    thin membranes that separate dimensions where
anything is possible and
        the least of all that is real is also probable.
They pose no threat to us, yet they
crush planets, suns and star systems absorbing them,
dwarfing them;

59

they bat at ticking neutron stars like little balls with bells.

But they still pose no threat to us.
They're just doing what billions of billions of kittens would do.
And we want to play with them as well:
to rub against their singularity and
                                        claim it as our own;
to see the light that cannot escape the event of
                                        our own horizon;
and if we could, we would witness **everything**
between our feet and
the still collective of those billions of billions of kittens
                                        way out there...
If we could truly see, we would witness
just how small we really are.

Maybe one day we'll be as big as them.
We will no longer seek only the comforts of
                                        living room carpets.
We'll be grown up cats prancing under the clean air of
                                        unblemished ozone.
We will walk confidently in lighted rooms
                          in palaces made of unity,
built on foundations solid in harmonies of
        songs sung by the ancient gods themselves.
We will properly fear our ignorance
(but still choose to gently poke at Ursa Major).
We will feel grateful and humbled for
the stars we roll around in the palms of our hands and
                                        ask for nothing in return.

We will be a billion cats safely illuminating
                                lazy summer beaches
and one day, far... far off into our ever expanding future,
we will collide with all that we could wish to be.
    We will venture into the great divide between
ignorance and I and we...
                        and we will become!

Like billions of billions of kittens we
won't cry over the sweeping arms
of the Milky Way,
            spilt way out there.

We won't fret plastic waste and worry
about sore paws that can't do enough
to make things the way
                        they ought to be.

We won't hiss and bat each other on the head
to protect a scrap of petroleum.
We will remember the ancient law that

            we are all of one litter,

because we'll be all grown up and in love with
                everything.
We'll run on sturdy legs,
                racing gravitational waves to
                        the center of
                                every galaxy...

But for now, we are still too small.
We are only the power of one kitten.
We are weak, but fearless.
We have power enough to end a war
to divert one when we're lucky –
power enough to start one when we're not–
We have kitten ideals
            not yet fully developed.
We are **one** kitten
            clutching lives like balls of yarn
with frayed ends twisting to the
                        end of this story...
We are not as big as we feel.
We are not big yet.

            But we are growing!

On Being
A Man

Fate didn't draw me this way, you did.
You wanted my lines carved from stones
      thrown by accusations and humiliations
      demanding I be more than any boy is capable.
But I didn't want to be more.
More than what?
More than natural reactions to things that break my chest?
No, I did not weep.
I fixed my expression,
      felt the warmth beneath the flesh on my face,
      puffed out my broken chest,
      grinned like a man and said things like,
          "Life goes on."

You wanted the boy I was to grow into a man, big and strong.
I did not want to be stronger.
Stronger than what?
Than the raw release of anguish?
Stronger than the twisted knots in my gut that
      existed because I was filled with fear.
You demanded I prove myself able to withstand
      the enormity of how I felt because
      you had to prove it too.
You made me destroy genuine honesty because
      yours was cracked and withered and
      lost, somewhere deep in your own childhood
No, I wanted to be weak:
      to find my strength within the agility of my soul.
      to be weak enough to be afraid,
         but go forward anyway.
A sacred little boy with the strength
      of my loved ones – of my tribe –
      to stand me up tall.
I wanted a tribe.

I did not want to stand alone.
A lone wolf, an impressive cliché just like
      every other real man.
A solo warrior bent on domination and destruction until
      I would be the last man standing.
The last man standing all alone, with
      no one to see how great I could be.
No, I wanted you with me.
I needed hearts that would hear the melody of:
      my joy, my sad, my courage, my fear.
I needed touches and caresses and smiles.
I would pave my path with the kind words and generosity of
      you who have loved me until
      my shell weakened
         and I became softer.

I did not want to be harder.
To have my lines etched
      from ideas of permanence in stone, or steel.
To have a countenance that could withstand
      typhoons and broken hearts –
      unbroken, and unmoved.
I needed to be moved.
I needed to flow with the tides of idea,
      to flow with lines of poetry.
I needed flexibility,
      like the surface of a teardrop just before
      it falls to the ground,
         breaking into smaller versions of itself.
I needed to be moldable, unfixed in my positions, because
      my mind explored the crevasses of imagination
      and when I saw a new thing,
         I became a new thing and
      would not have been able to
         had I been so fixed in the mold you made for me.

I did not want to "be a man".
But, I became an animal:
      primal and rabid,

running unstoppable streets,
destroying innocence wherever I found it –
I was a cold statue of a man,
         occupying a child's body...

I did not want to "be a man!"
I wanted to rage against your demands.
I wanted to be free from the prison you constructed from my
bones.
I wanted to destroy what you made me.
I wanted to destroy me.
I wanted me.
I wanted me.
I just wanted to be.

Spotted

She sits alone at the base of the hill
across the little rocky creek.
Brown hide spotted with tenderness,
she also could be a he.
They take a casual step, bound in innocence:
meek, graceful, free.
Their gaze climbs the hillside made of snow
spotted with tufts of sage.
So far away the top of the hill seems
for such a little thing,
but they jump and bounce up the slope
because they spotted me.

Soles

This is my meditation:
I bought a new pair of shoes –
     more than I could afford
     but worth it for the brand:
         known, trusted
         tested on celebrity athletes.
Must have value?
They replaced my old pair of shoes which cost
     a few bucks on a whim,
     and fit my funny fat feet with ease,
     but suffered trauma
     tromping to far on rocky dirt trails:
         their soles had worn smooth,
         though still enough soul to reach a peak.
My old soles have no holes.

The new shoes – each one – split down the sides
     before I had time to
         learn how to love them
           (and they me).
It didn't take long at all until they were
     spilling me into puddles,
     slipping down dusty trails,
     gasping for air.
They had a terrible time making it to the peak!
I only wanted to break them in, but
     they just broke.
They were there because my old shoes
     retired with dignity.

So, I bought another new pair of shoes on a whim
     for just a few bucks.
Same brand as my old shoes, but
     a different name.
They are hard and painful.
They are cold an inflexible.
They will not tear, but will not run.

They care nothing for the trail.
Nothing for my feet.
Nothing for me.

In despair, I sat on a bench wishing.
I wanted to be on the trail.
In the midst of my sadness,
I bowed my head to weep and took in the sight of my bare
feet.
They looked strong,
ready to run, to skip, to dance beyond the peaks
of my trials and carry me to wherever
        my path lay.
My feet had no tears.
They wanted me as much as I wanted good shoes.

I took off my shoes and let my feet feel
        the dust and rocks and
                they were ok with
                        with the state of the trail.

So we walked on…
        sometimes in pain...
        sometimes in ease...
                depending on shape of the trail…

Eventually, I bought more shoes and
        tried them on the trail.
Some of them enjoyed the hike;
        some enjoyed the run;
                some just wanted carpet and linoleum.
But whatever shoes I wore,
        my feet – my steadfast, reliable feet –
        were always what took me where
                I needed be.

There's No Place Like Localhost

I'm trapped in a box of bits and there's no way out.

I am defined as the Licensee in every End User License Agreement available.

That is who I've become.

Let me warn you, never trust Tech Support when they tell you that the error is an ID-TEN-T, because no tech support associate has ever spelled number.

I have become the ghost in the machine because I cannot read the data-stream fast enough.

I cause bottlenecks serial bandwidths and I have to put on hip-waders to shovel out the bitwise sludge.

I administer licensed software across a network of hundreds of nodes wondering if some machine has a dysfunctional NIC or a bad CAT5, but I'd rather stand under a summer sun and let the rays massage my nerves.

I want to write poetry on the server room walls, but I can't because I'm stuck in a database between a clock-in and a clock-out timestamps. MySQL owns me for 28,800,000 milliseconds every day.

I want to get this stupid upgrade finished but people keep calling me because some obscure program won't open... I know how to install it but I don't know what it does.

It gives an error that reads, "Windows cannot find the file specified. A corrupted bit might be causing a memory leak or maybe your day-life just sucks that bad. It is suggested in the most passive voice possible that perhaps if you knew what you were doing the author of this error wouldn't have to tell you to check the minimum requirements on page 523 of the installation guide. Close unnecessary hopes and dreams and try installing the program again. If you continue to receive this message, please call tech support at 1-800-go-fucking-kill-yourself-no-one-would-ever-notice."

I want to go home, but I'm trapped in an IP address of 127.0.0.1. There's no place like localhost. There's no place like localhost.
My daylife is a 404 error – page not found.
The page is not found because I haven't found the space to write it.
And it would not be a Wiki-doc
You couldn't google it or bing it or cite it or love it or... or...

There are days when everything works harmoniously. A room full of Dell Optiplex 9010's emits a soft hush from synchronized CPU fans. Users crowd over clacking keyboards and swishing mice absorbed in AutoCAD or Photoshop without complaint. Over the low din through an open window, you can hear the squawking chatter of magpies, a distant lawnmower rowing through a green-sea lawn, or the siff-slip-clap of flip-flops on concrete.

I can sit on a bench outside and have a smoke and point my face at the sun and close my eyes and breathe. I can take a moment, think about a joke I read in a chat room and laugh out loud using my real voice. I can slouch on the grass against a tree and dream about poetry.

But today, I'm trapped in a box of bits and there's no way out.

I Breathe

I breathe... slowly.
I breathe slowly and the world melts away.
This is my in-breath... this is my out-breath.
This is my in-breath and it nourishes my body.
This is my out-breath and it cleanses my mind.

On the first breath, my chest feels heavy, weighed down by
      surface distractions making demands
      on my optic nerves, but
                  then I exhale.
The many-languaged voices in this airport terminal begin to fade with
      the falling light of day through the window behind me.
Running-child footsteps clomp to a beat
      establishing a rhythm backed up by
      the mechanical clip-clap of the baggage claim.
The cell-phone confessionals surrounding the giant hall begin a chorus.

I take a second breath and my chest feels heavy still, now weighed down by
      all the things that want to keep me up at night:
      more bills than paychecks,
      getting old,
      the daily changing view in the mirror,
      the half-broken car,
      loneliness,
      dying alone...
                  but then I exhale.
Suddenly, I am able to be happy to have food and a roof and a toilet;
      a transient walks by with
      a smile and a nod he's saved all day just for me.
I remember playing with my nephew's dog this morning and
      the glee she gave freely to me;
I remember the other day when I looked in the mirror and for a moment thought,

"I look pretty damn good right now!"
I remembered the five dollars in my pocket that could buy me a tea if I wanted.
A woman walked by with a frown on her face and a crinkled brow and
> *when her eyes met mine I smiled and nodded*
> *like I had been saving it all day for just her,*
> *and then she smiled back and stood up just a little taller.*

I take a third breath, and the weight begins to lessen.
The dance of passers-by become a well-constructed choreography.
Children transform from beasts to superheroes, to unicorns, and mermaids.
I feel the corners of my mouth stretch and
> *watch the traveling smile widen as it moves from face to*
face.
I see apologetic laughter between strangers bumping bags.
Handshakes between surprised friends crossing paths to different destinations.

I take another breath, and the weight is gone.
My shoulders feel relaxed and the happy din around me slowly fades.
Now I see my thoughts, like miniature movies on the backs of my eyelids.
I see resistance to the quiet as ego listens for noise to fill the newfound void.

I take another breath and the sounds fade away.
I feel the constant beat of my heart in my chest, my wrists, my ears.

Another breath.
I am light.
I am calm.
I can feel my feet touching the floor beneath me.
It is solid and I am grateful.

I Fall in Love

I saw a meme on Facebook that told me to think about
    all the times I've fallen in love and

never said a word.
So I thought about it.
The thing about me is,
      I fall in love with someone new
      at least twice every single day:
-- all ten of the Yogi-Writers on Elephant Journal
      who wrote about me what women want...
-- the woman in the martial arts class with
      the lumberjack punch that shook my ribs...
-- every woman with a tattoo habit...
-- the woman in line in front of me at the grocery store.
      we had almost the same items in our carts but
      I ate an awesome salad alone that night...
-- the roller derby queen...
-- the punk rock vixen...
-- the artist, the singer, the drama queen, the dancer who
      tried in vain to show me how to get down
      because she had such a great laugh...
-- the woman with the smile, the woman with the eyes,
      the woman walking her dog, lost in thought,
      smiling at her musings...
-- the quiet one in the corner of the library who
      bit her lip and melted my whole world
      into oblivion as she read her book so responsively...
-- the angel who almost t-boned my car and
      mouthed, "I'm so sorry" when our eyes met...
That is my list for this week, so far...

This is just who I am.
I was born under a Venusian sun, ruled by the Goddess of
Love.
But then that meme said there are that many people who
      have fallen in love with me
      and never said a word.

I dismissed THAT right away!
I mean, obviously this faceless meme didn't know
      me very well, right?
I mean, I'm the guy that always wants, but

72

is never wanted.
I'm the guy, with the great sense of humor,
        if you're twelve.
The guy, the old guy, the bald guy, over-sensitive guy...
The broke guy, the broken guy, the guy with
        the broken down SUV...
The bad teeth, bad back, bad style,
        the guy with the bad past
        that permanently etched in his brain
        at childhood
        that he's just bad bad bad...
The self-conscious guy that sucks in his gut, hides his smile,
        hides fear behind wit.

What countless number of people would fall in love
        with the guy that can't dance
        and never say anything?
The guy that can't --
        no matter how many hours at the gym each day --
        shed this final layer of belly fat.
The guy living in the broken down trailer.
The guy with the GoodWill wardrobe.
The guy with the lowest available salary in the highest paid
line of work.
The guy that spends all his free time writing bad poetry.
The guy that loves too deeply...
The guy that loves much too deeply...

I saw another meme today,
        a quote by Rumi,
He says that   what we seek,   seeks us.

            and it made me think:

what is it that is seek?   I think I

        just want to be loved for who I am   and

        it hit me,   who I truly seek is   me...

73

Wyatt Always-Forward

Wyatt is a punk rocker:
>beat
>broken
>ground into the dust of the long and lonely road
>but still
>immortal,
>indestructible:

He called me over and over until I answered.
It was almost a year since I shouldn't have survived
>my suicide.
But Wyatt had just found out a few minutes ago.

"Everything tries to kill you, every day, Kelly…"
He says this to me from deep in the Smoky Mountains
>on his latest quest to walk the entire length of the
>Appalachian Trail
"But you push-the-fuck-on…"
>More than 300 miles and three months
>since he took a selfie at the trailhead,
>and he tells me how precious life is
>that it all happens on the trail,
>not at the peak,
>not at the end,
>not by giving up because it's too hard,
>not by avoiding the scary shit,

"It's in the sweat and stink,"
Wyatt says,
"It's under a tarp, alone in the pitch black of deep night,
>on the top of a strange mountain
>with pellets of frozen rain sneering
>at your mortality."
"Always forward,"
I hear conviction drip from his lips,
through missing teeth and vodka breath.

"It's in surviving the bullet you fed yourself for dessert
        when life force-fed you the death of your only son –
"It's in laughing through the headaches inoperable
        tumors squeeze into your fucking brain;
        you belly laugh when the doctor tells you
        six weeks left –
"Always forward,"
        he says this without an ounce of desperation –
        I would be desperate –
        but with reverence for something so precious as
        life
"It's in never taking it for granted, brother,
        not even when the doctors tell you
        cancer is eating your body like it's a fucking twinkie, no,
        you   fucking   push   on,"

All I can think is that there is a father alone in the mountains
without a child in this world,
living with death like an annoying acquaintance
that you wish would just go bug someone
someone else for a change...

He tells me how valuable I am...
He tells me how strong I am...
How much of an inspiration and role model
        I've been to him...

"Always forward,"
        he says, and I have no choice but to obey,
        because what excuses do I have in this conversation?
        My little fears are small things?

Discussion: Changing Perspective

I read in a book one time four words that sent tingles up my spine, "Changing perspective changes perception." Until that moment, shifting my perspective sometimes seemed impossible. I couldn't think my way out of thought patterns that could ultimately prove destructive. These four words gave me a new way of looking with intent, and ultimately, became magic that I could capture in poetry.

What is perception?

Let's answer this very simply: perspective is what you can see from where you are. Take a second and look at the world in front of you. Everything that you can see is available for you to perceive. Everything that you hear, smell, taste, touch from right where you are is what you can perceive.

Your perceptions are more accurate when you can use all your senses, but if a smell wafts from behind you, you have to use your imagination to fill in the gaps... unless you turn your head.

What is perspective?

It is the place from which you observe. When you turned your head to investigate the smell from behind you and discovered a hot dog cart, you connected the smell to the source. Turning your head changed your perspective.

So?

You have power over your perspective, but your available perceivable experiences are completely limited by your current perspective. We don't have very much power over our perceptions.

Caveat: we never truly perceive all there is to perceive from our current perspective, so exploring our current perspective is valuable! Our immediate perspective is the only place we can capture a moment (Chapter 4 discusses capturing a moment).

However, we can get trapped in a perception if we are not careful (i.e. core beliefs, judgmentalism, negative self-assessment, etc). And there are plenty of trapped perceptions within us.

Using Poetry Magic to Change Perspective

On Being a Man is one of my favorite poems to discuss for this topic. Growing up as a white, hetero, cis-male in the 80s and 90s, was not conducive to breaking out of the trap our misogynistic, homophobic, patriarchal culture had set up for me. I knew at age 17 that I did not want to be what was expected of me.

But I didn't have very many possible perspectives from which to perceive what it was that I wanted to be. It took years of floundering and identifying then attacking internal beliefs before I understood how these social beliefs didn't only hurt people within minority groups, but they hurt everyone. They hurt me.

Switching from the perspective of chipping away at the core beliefs given to me by my culture, to the perspective of healing myself from cultural trauma gave me a new way to look at the issue. On Being a Man was a poem cast from that new perspective.

They were no longer my beliefs (nor shame, nor guilty), but a sickness that can be cured with love!

Practice

Let's look at something (light) from a different perspective!

1) Find something around you that you find beautiful.
2) Move to a place where it fills your perspective and you can focus on it.
3) Write a few lines describing it as you are experiencing it.
4) Now, switch your perspective internally! Stop thinking about the object, but about its history. Write down a few things about where it came from. How far back do you want to go? What/who made it?
5) Write a poem from your new perspective.
6) When your satisfied with the poem you just cast, write it in the spaces provided in the next couple pages.

Chapter 4: Capturing a Moment

Magic never exists in the past or the future. It only happens within this moment. Poetry Magic gives us the power of capturing a moment, and thus capturing the Voice of Healing that fills the infinite space therein.

That magic, manifested in the form of a poem can be released an infinite number of times and never be depleted. In fact, it grows when tapped into.

The Smile

When she walks, she smiles like no one is looking.
There is narrative there.
A story for her lover, about her lover.
Behind that smile, in the spaces where
        her thoughts are hers alone,
        she fills them with thoughts of him
        and she would not pollute them with
        language,
        so she says everything in the
        stretch of her lips.
Her eyes, cast to the ground –
        not because she's sad,
        but because the things in the world
        around her that she could see are
        too mundane to reflect any
        spectrums brilliant enough
        to share space with her wordless thoughts of love.
No, she casts her eyes down to paint
        memories on the floor of moments ago, when
        she felt her lovers lips;
        when she felt her lovers embrace;
        when she met her lovers gaze and saw
        her own reflected there.

If moments are infinite, her smile and her downcast eyes
    become the universe in which she exists.
If moments are fleeting, she paints infinite joys
    on their smooth, wanting surfaces;
If they are fleeting she etches infinite poems on them
    with her smile and
    her downcast eyes.
Fleeting moments repeat and multiply, surrounding her
    with all the grace of a dervish
    who never tired of being
    the beloved and the lover.
Fleeting moments take up the space of a heartbeat –
    a hard beat,
    pushing on the edges
    like veins swollen with dopamine,
    pulsing with infatuation,
    throbbing with moments filled with
    recent memories of her lovers lips and
    seeing herself reflected in his gaze...

Her reverie won't be interrupted in this lifetime.

Late Coming Spring

Small wispy clouds passing nervously by,
"Don't mind me, just on my way through."
Wandering weather wondering whether
winter will leave the ground.

Cold frozen creek mostly covered in ice
coat unbuttoned most of the way.
"Don't look at me, man, this isn't your plan."
as he's trying to keep his cool.

Bare naked tree showing more than just thigh
feigning not noticing an ogling magpie
desperate for the touch of a new lover
who will ride in on rays of summer sun.

Slow moving breaths shivering
through bare branch forests before
dissipating into some forgotten dimension
beyond eyesight and hindsight.

Sunshine wanting warmth it cannot
find inside the atoms of cold
where ions fuse with suppressed longings
for a Spring coming too late.

A young doe scratching crusty
drifts of winter showing signs
of aging – having lived beyond
expected life spans – for nourishment.

It all ends when Robin steals a twig
to make her nest on low branches
where her babes will not fall too far
in just a couple months.

My Backyard

This chair only moves when rain or snow
threaten a wet ass or a need to stand.
This is the spot where fear and frustrations
are swept downstream if only for a minute.
The spot where great ideas grow like the
natural grass lawn that hasn't been watered
since 1989 -- there's been enough rain since
then.
This is where I wait for the morning sun
to sweep me off into the reality that daytime
usually thrusts upon my unwilling shoulders.
This is where a smoke and a cup of coffee is
best.

From this spot I can watch eternity frame
a hawk riding currents and a fat beaver
bask his fat belly by the fat creek bank and
then
find a new home downstream or maybe up.
I can watch a fawn grow and make more
fawns.
Bald eagles spread massive black wings
as they leave branchy perches for other trees.
Bears warily flop running feet rapidly so close
to a man.

This is where I usually sit when squawky duck
couples
float against lazy currents of clear water
covering green rocks that are surprisingly not
slippery.
So much happens here, but this back yard
isn't very big.

Where Life

Where the horizon hides
between
sea and clouds
 ablaze with passion...

Where the stars are as
bright as your desire...

Where water retreats,
 exposing the sand
 as if to greet bare feet with
 royal bows and curtsies...
 Where bare skin prickles with
 freedom under a sky dome
slowly   becoming divided
   by bright milky trails --
these skies seems so small, and
          so far away, but to see them
          must mean you are as infinite as
          the Universe and
          as powerful as the grains of sand that
          clinging to your feet memories you
          wish to keep forever.
Where lovers look into each other's eyes with
wonder – not familiarity –
       and every shared moment feels like
       exploring a new planet, or like
       re-reading your favorite story for the first time
Where the daytime air is filled with calm smiles on

strangers' faces,
      and sleep comes as simply as the constant,
      rhythmic lullaby-drone of the sea,
      and everything...
            just...
                  slows...
                        down...

This is where I want to build sandcastles with
      savory views of deep blues and
      seaweed landscaping big enough for
      family playtime,
      reading poetry,
      writing love stories,
      making love,
      making lives that last an eternity...

I watched the setting sun ignite the hidden line
between sea and sky.
The explosion seared my tension and
      I felt a smile I've worn before return,
      oneI had not felt mold my lips in so long....

This is not a place.
This is not a destination.
I carry it in my ribs.
It sits at the bottom of my pocket.
I wear it in my shoe for good luck.
It tickles my neck.
It is the Will of the Universe.
It is a single moment.
It is all moments.
It is my heart.
It is my spirit.
It is who I became when the tide came back in.

She danced on the first warm day of Spring,
　　　twirling like a dervish with arms spread wide,
　　　head tilted to the side with
　　　her face turned upward
　　　toward the warmth she adored,
　　　toward the sunshine craved since
　　　　　the first cold winter day.

Her feet were bare, lightly touching the
　　　damp ground now finally soft from thaw.

Winter, finally passed, gave way to a late spring,
　　　renewed vigor, and reawakened bliss.
　Songbirds sung again:
　　　songs of remembrance,
　　　of new hopes,
　　　of bright, sunny days to come,
　　　songs of becoming drunk on
overripe berries and
　　　ecstacy,
　　　songs impassioned
with joy and anticipation
　　　of fat worms climb-
ing up from beneath the
　　　　soft earth.

Their lyrics did not penet-
rate her ears, but
　　　she felt them
　　　with her body and
　　　she moved her body
　　　with them in response.

The First Warm

She felt the sunshine touch her skin through her
light spring dress and
the sun's warm rays gently kissed her neck
like the slow, breathy kisses of
a generous and patient lover.
When her body moved,
she simply let go and
let it move as it desired...

In that moment, she lived within the balances
between her spirit and
the revelation of summer forthcoming;

Day of Spring

between her
fantasies and
the embrace of her
lover;

between living
and
being
alive...

The Secret Life of the Lunch Lady

She spends her day locked away in the back of a kitchen.
She makes the food you and I take for granted:
        unattributed to caring hands.
In the sunlight,
        she has no face,
        no smile,
        no form...
You neither love nor hate the food she makes,
        but it nourishes you;
        it gets you through the day.
And if you are the fortunate type of person that
        thinks about where your food comes from,
        maybe you are grateful
        for the hands and heart that made it.

But hold on!
She doesn't want you to feel guilty for forgetting her.
Recognition is not her calling.
Cooking is not her calling.
That's just how she pays the bills.

But...
Her life
        when the sun goes down...
                that's...
                        where...
                                she lives!
It's where she comes alive.
It's the music though which she moves her body,
        through which her body moves.
Where she faces stranger's eye to eye to
        see into you
                as she moves.
As rapid, island beats fill her soul with Ja and Love
        she smiles, and dances;
                she kicks her feet with joy,

she pumps her arms with ecstasy,
she bends at the hips with
         repetitive flexibility found only in Rasta rhythms.

Though surrounded by the crowd,
       she dances alone,
       whether or not the music is playing – sometimes,
               she dances to the memory of rhythm.
She doesn't sweat, because
       it's not about that.
It's not about working hard, or
       fighting for the struggle, man.
It's about the presence of God
       whose hands reach out for her
       whose hands caress her
               tightly in a grip of Love, and so
               she simply allows the grip to move her,
       move her,
move her along the scuffed, beer-stained, hardwood floor:
       splotchy shades of old dust and booze...

She makes the band smile, and
       turns the volume in their voices up,
       the beats on the drums up,
       the deep lyrics of the bass up,
       the joyful squeals of the saxophone up,
       the mood of the room
       up….
               up…
                       up...
They are all so high.
So high above the daily grind,
       above the faultless blameless
               ignorance of her existence, she moves.
She moves through the illusion of strangers,
       through the other dancers

peppering the floor she shares with them
and the illusion of strangers fades
behind their faces and
they become known to her.
She searches pairs of eyes where friends and lovers hide
and finds them widely smiling,
sometimes singing along,
clapping away the ends of songs,
oblivious to her...
She recognizes transformations congregating in
shared surprise and raucous laughter,
the kind that comes pleasantly surprised at
sudden hilarity.

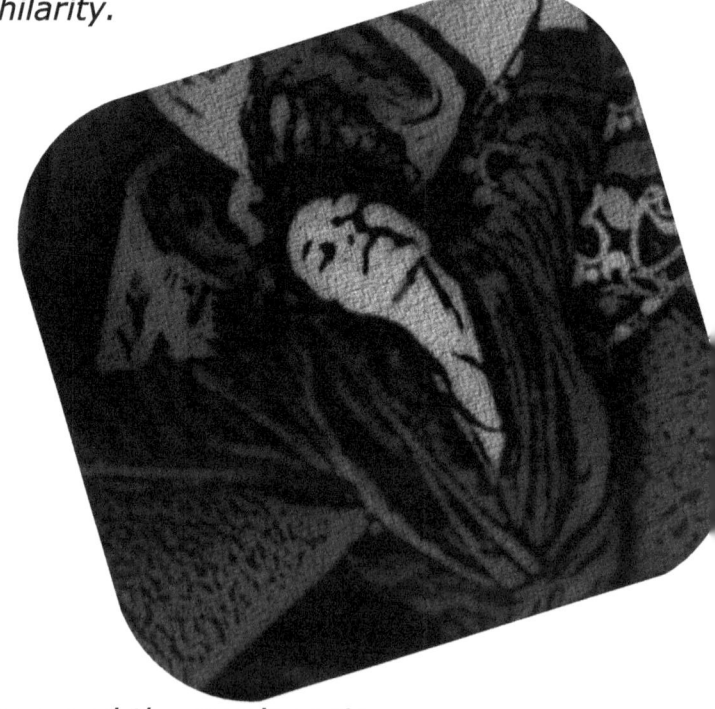

When the night is done and the music rests,
she travels lightly to her apartment, where
she sits quietly in the dark,
moving her shoulders to
the memory of Rasta Rhythms.
In the morning, the sun will come back up and
she will make us our food, and
we won't know how she moves.

Discussion: Capturing a Moment

Magic does not happen in the future or the past. It happens in this, and only this, moment. When writing Magic Poetry, that is where we need to exist.

Past and Future

A most magnificent thing that Poetry Magic has taught me is that the past and future are both limited by my imagination. It isn't possible to remember the past perfectly, and it is silly to place an expectation on my imagined future (I know, easier said than done). These imaginings are very limited versions of reality. The constraints they place around the past and the future exclude infinite possibilities of experience, perspective and perception.

Yes, we can absolutely find magic in these imaginings. They are, after all, creations of our Creative Self, and (as we learned in Chapter 1) that is where our power to heal lives.

Please do not think I am discouraging use of memory and imagination of the future. These are sacred and valuable forms of energy. Exploring the limitations of these constructs is also quite valuable.

One last point to consider: poetry can be about memories or hopes/fears, but the magic is woven when the words are put to page... in this moment.

Welcome to this moment

When I am alive and aware in this moment, the power my imagination has to put constraints on any experience is only perceptual. Every experience in the Universe is available to me. I have the freedom here to move.

I can change my perspective.

Capturing this moment

When I try to explain this concept, I use the first poem in this chapter, The Smile, as my example.

I was sitting in a busy dining room, waiting for a moment to capture, when I saw a woman stand up from a table in my line of view. She suddenly smiled; it was a very specific type of smile (this was the moment I captured). I followed the direction of her gaze towards the entrance and there was a man walking toward us, wearing the same smile. She walked toward him and when they met, they kissed.

What happened to me in that moment was that I recognized that smile. I have worn it before. It was the mutual recognition experienced by two lovers when their eyes meet. That is what I tried to capture from that perception, within that perspective, of that moment. The magic, was the recognition of the experience. You see, I was allowed to feel the emotions of sudden joy, excitement, anticipation, and love even though I wasn't the one making that connection.

Magic!

Practice

Now it's your turn! You're going to go hunting for a moment to capture. Try this practice with focused intent:

1) Prepare the things you need and make sure you have them at the ready (i.e. notepad and pencil/pen, laptop/tablet/phone, anything you usually use to write on/with).

2) Go somewhere you enjoy. Be it a cafe, a busy park or a quiet one, somewhere you can sit within nature, somewhere you think you might enjoy having an experience. Find a place to exist where you can see and experience things you enjoy seeing and experiencing.

3) It helps me sometimes to bring sage or incense and ritualize my internal preparation when possible. If I'm indoors, I'll bring my runes and have a quick casting before I begin hunting. Whatever you think will help put your mindset into a creative internal space. Anything that will help you hear your intuition a little more clearly.

4) Now sit and wait. Look around. Try not to engage with your environment; just be an observer. Try not to engage with your internal narratives – don't try to stop them, just don't engage. We want those narratives. One of them will eventually speak loudly, pointing to your moment. You'll feel some emotions stronger than others. If it is a profound recognition, you might even feel goosebumps. You'll know when you have found your moment. It will feel much like, "Aha!"

5) Write one phrase describing what triggered the moment. No more than a sentence. Those will be the trigger words for your poem. As you're writing, you'll look back to this phrase for fuel.

6) Don't wait! The moment is slipping by! Turn it into a poem and write it down. Let your words flow as they come out (there will be time to edit/revise if needed later). Get it all out. Tell the Universe what you experienced.

7) Feel the Magic you just created.

8) Share it! Write it in the space provided on the next two pages.

Thank you for sharing this experience with me!

Chapter 5: Learning to Love

Love is not just a feeling, but an action. In fact, it is far more something we do than it is something we feel. This does not diminish the raw power of the emotion, but by itself the emotion is only within us and does not affect the world around us. The emotion compels us to take action (i.e. choosing to spend time with someone), but it is when we love with the intention to Love that we create powerful energy.

Loving intentionally can take a lifetime of learning and evolving. Poetry Magic can help us harness the power of Love and heal ourselves as well as others.

My Little Monster

I never had an inner child.
Mine was an inner little monster.
And though I love him desperately...
    he doesn't know I exist.

He crouches in the darkest corners of my psychology,
    keeping guard...
      from chance encounters with kind strangers,
      my little monster keeps a silent watch.
He looks for warm smiles like mortal threats –
    his hackles rise at heartfelt gestures
    and he wants so desperately to be left alone...
      almost as much as he wants to be held...
      not as much as he wants to feel wanted...
      by some strange type of love that is
        safe from ever being ripped away;

...he is convinced no such love exists,
        except:
                I love him that much...

He is Feral.
He weeps quietly behind my eyes when I'm smiling.

His sobs resonate like symphonies,
        like requiems lamenting the inevitable
                deaths of genuine connections –
                        permanent endings –
        filled spaces always drain into
                an infinite void where only
                        nothing
                                can exist.
I try to show him every day

                – Every! Day! –
        that the Universe is made primarily of Love,
        and the empty spaces are not trying to be empty,
but
        are reserved for the love yet to come –
        and I try to show him that it is, in fact, coming.

I pause at morning pastel pinks and blues
         that linger above the Bridger Mountains
         to revel in the love nature has for art,
                  but he knows the sun will soon
                  paint over it all with washed-out yellows.
So I show him how the Sun loves warmth
         with gentle strokes of sunshine on his cheek,
         but he recoils in fear of being burned,
         convinced he will be consumed and forgotten...

         So I try to show him how to be loved when
                  she looks at me intently, tickling
                  my soul, igniting my heart...
But he shields his eyes from the flame,
         covers his ears to the exchange of shared
sentiments
                  because he doesn't believe in fairy tales
         and if they were real,
                  he is convinced he is
                           the pea,
                                    the glass slipper,
                                             the poison
                                                      apple...

                  How do you love a little monster
                           who is so terrified of love?
                  He has taught me over the years,
                  that
                           the only way to tame with
                  love is that
                                    you just don't stop...
                                             ...ever...

99

My Fears are Real!

Let's talk about fear.
Have you ever heard someone say that
F.E.A.R is just False Evidence Appearing Real?
I'm not convinced.

Like when you're lying in bed,
> just about asleep when you feel that
> tickle
> travel along the back of your shoulder,
> like feather fingers brushing your skin,
> but really fucking fast and you know it's a spider,
> so you jump up and brush it away,
> knowing that touching it with your hand
> will make it bite you!

Then, after you feel that burning sting on your back
> in a spot you know you won't
> be able to see –
>> though you twist neck sideways trying anyway –
> you realize: what if it was a motherfucking black widow, or
> a brown recluse, or
> some other demon born
> eight-eyed, eight-legged, hairy, creepy-crawly,
>> death bringing devil bug?

So you search in the area you think you flung the damned thing,
> tearing apart your bed,
> stumbling on a pillow,
> falling face-fucking-first into the wall and
> letting out a half panic, half rage scream that
> turns the neighbor's light on.

Sleep doesn't really come again, but
> in the morning, you check your shoulder in the mirror and
> there isn't anything there at all and
> you can't feel precisely where the bite wound was...

Ok, that's a bad example, but...

What about that feeling you get when you see the

red and blue lights in your rear-view mirror and
you realize you have no idea how fast you're going so
you jerk your foot away from the accelerator and
realize there is nowhere to pull off and the next turn is
          too far down the road to resemble anything like
a comfortable place to meet a cop,
so you speed up to get to it faster but
then realize the cop might think you're evading, and
          you don't want to make local headlines
for being involved in a high-speed chase so you
slow down again and just stop!

Just...
stop...
on the shoulder and
try not to drive into the ditch
but the cop just passes you
on his way to his actual target.

Wait, wait... I have a better example...

Like when your socially awkward brother texts you,
          "I have news cant talk now call you later" and
          doesn't use any punctuation,
          or emojis and won't return your text so
          you have no context to decide if it's good news or
          bad news or
          boring news or
          if it's going to just be a big fat fucking lie
          because he's done this a few times before and
          it was sometimes good news and sometimes bad news and

          last time it was to tell you that your grandmother
          was in a horrible accident,
          and when you called your dad,
          he had no clue, but would see if he could figure it out and
          after you texted your sister who didn't know anything and
          then your dad texts you back saying
          your uncle doesn't know anything either,
          and now there are cousins and facebook and

101

emails and texts flying all over the internet and
your brother finally gets back to you two hours later to
tell you he had a job interview at a grocery store
close to where he lived so it would be really convenient and

help him save gas money.

Ok, so sometimes, maybe fear is not really all that real,
But sometimes, it's very real.

Like when she smiles at you in that way she does
just before she tilts her head back to laugh and
you want to pull her close to you and
look deeply into her eyes,
tell her she's beautiful,
that you think you might love her,
but the words just don't come out and
your hands are stuck in your jeans pockets.
Maybe you shouldn't say anything, because,
what if she gets disgusted and walks away.
What if she walks out of your life forever and
hates you for complicating everything and
destroying your friendship?
What if she laughs and says, "I'm sorry, for a second I thought
you were serious."

And what if she pulls you into her, and
months go by and
years go by and
you find out the hard way that
she never liked your inner-child; that,
she just got used to you and...

Sometimes, my fears are real.
Always, they are just fear...

Tandem

I am within you   I am with you   I am
   you

I watch you from above your space of perception.
You have sensed me...
And I've not hidden from you, but
   my voice has always be just below
       a whisper in the din, or
       a thought passing just below
         worry...
I was there, always, reaching you quietly through
   all the worry, fear, obsession, anxiety;
   I was there.

You've heard my voice,
and sought me,
not knowing who I was...

Please know, I have always known you.

I am within you   I am with you   I am
   you

When you fell, I was panic;
When you worried, I was imagination;
When you laughed, I was whimsy;

I remember the day you let the cold rain sting your
   cheek,
lost in obsession and isolation:
   You felt you were alone,
   That no one could hear your voice,
      But I did.
   I was the gentleness of pity that you so
   desperately needed.
   You tried to think that you would never be loved,

but
    I loved you...
I held your heart in my hand and,
        hoping they would bring warmth,
    I let my tears fall gently
            into the wounds.

I am within you   I am with you   I am
    you

When you panicked, I was courage.
When you Imagine, I become poetry.
When you played, I was joy.

And I remember the day you raised your head to the
    top of the mountain;
    You said to the world that
            you would make it to the top...
                and then you did!
    I was the pride you discovered there,
            the soreness in your feet,
    I was the wow you found at doing impossible
    things;
        I became the drive to do it again,
                and again...
    We made that peak together so many times that I
    became
            your expectation of achievement, and
                we never let each other down.

I am within you   I am with you   I am
    you

When you loved, you were me.
When you wept, I was you.
When you sought me, I sought you.

When you found me, we became the Universe...

Waiting for Portraits

I sit
and wait
for portraits to appear...

and as my breath reflects shapes
of soft spring winds
that whisper
secrets
through pine wood scents
        in places I recalled
                when I became Spring,

I felt my body sway, and I thought of an angel
        wearing a monster suit.
My heart still breaks for her from time to time,
        but this poem is not about her.

But it has not broken for my self in several lifetimes –
        I have become my breath;
        I have remembered my connections
        to Spring.

I think of all the ways
        I've fallen...
And on my quest for the bottom of the bottom,
        I do not know when I learned to fly,
        but you should see me soar
        when I remember that I can...

I do not mean watch me;
what I mean is, you should join me,
because flying is not as complicated
as falling:
It takes a lifetime to learn to fall;
and a single moment to fly.

Today: I polished clouds with my smile
and stroked the sun's cheek and
I did not worry about melting my wings –
You see,
mine are not made of wax, but
precious gemstones collected
from every bottom I've ever hit.

I defied the laws of gravity and hovered above the
scents of pine wood secrets
and quietly rejoiced in a
type of knowing that:
cleared my lungs,
cleansed my blood,
polished my hope and joy,
and let the sunlight through my pupils.

I landed gently on the ground, letting my bare
feet
dance on the Earth's pulse,
reminding myself that the sun shines,
trees grow in their own time,
life passes by in flashes,
collected gemstones are not so easy to find,
and portraits are not made;
they are revealed.

She Blinked

She blinked and the Universe went dim.
My breath caught in a temporal freeze as
Creation waited for her to open them again.

When they did, I saw again
the reason for my existence.
What shone through them?
Her love for me.
Years of heartbreak painted in plastic on
A blue-grey canvas...

"I feel safe," she said.

I looked deeper into those vast moonfire ponds
and kissed away the plastic.

"You are safe," I replied.

I pulled her body close to mine.
I wanted to pull us into one another,
To wipe away the illusion of space,
To fill the mirage of distance with the burning
Of our souls,
To become one with those eyes…
Those eyes…
My Gods… those… eyes…

I pressed her harder against me,
Feeling every inch of her against every centimeter
Of me. She… lightly moaned.
I felt the vibration of her love
wash against my tongue,
rattle against the deepest parts of me;
my pulse raced the rattling moan
and my blood heated,
burning against self-control;

And then she blinked, and the Universe went dim.
When she opened her eyes,
I was gone.
A fantasy.
A wish.

To Write You as a Poem

Should write you as a poem on this page,
I would begin with young galaxies,
  deep, blue-grey pinwheels
  contained by the mysteries of space,
  than loom hypnotically,
  hiding every story I've ever wanted to hear.

I would paint with words a clear sky in late Spring
  warning of dusk, when
    the last sliver of sun hides
    just behind a mountain and
    the whole of Nature begins to
  settle from the toils of the day.

I would articulate a deep mountain spring pool of
  crystal clear water
  carved into rock over eons, and
    more beautiful by far beyond fairness to
    all things beautiful.

I would carve these things with
  ink and love to describe your eyes.
    and they would be inadequate...

I would then pen narratives of
  the type of joy expressed by dancing children
  when the music sings to the way
  their little bodies move with no inhibition.

I would capture the warmth of sunrays
  massaging cherry blossoms that were
  content on swaying in gentle breezes,
    but clinging steadfast to their branches
    because they love their trees
  and they love to dance.

I would describe the joy a wanderer lost in a
  desert must feel
  when discovering an oasis filled with
  ripe sweet fruit and deep pools of clean water.

I would inscribe these words on the fabric of
  infatuation to capture some essence of your
  smile
        but they would be inadequate...

And I would speak directly to those parts of you
  that doubt.
I would hold them close to my body and beg
  them to see you through
  my eyes, because if they did,
  you would never doubt anything ever again.

You would become lost in those eyes
  and the spirit behind them and become
  entranced.
You would burn with desire to
  taste the sweetness of your smile.
You would be blinded by the brilliance of
  your intellect and feel the burning in my gut
        for seeking meaning.
You would feel the urge in me to
  trace every line of your body with my hands.
You would find eternity passing through
  a moment
  when our lips touch and
  you would wish time would stop
        right there.

If I could write you on this page,
  you would be able to read the poetry
        I see.

But words would be inadequate

Primal

I sit in the epicenter
       – my old world now annihilated –
of my own rebirth into a new thing.

I am amid distant rushes of breezes and streams;
the low hum of ancient mountain song;
the crackle of campfire burning on passion;
the chatter of songbirds singing secrets
       to a forest that sits in audience, watching
       clouds imitate the sharp granite peaks
       surrounding this great bowl.
I am no longer of the world of men;
I belong to the wild;
I am ready
to be consumed
by Gaia...

I feel the breeze – her breath – kiss my shoulder, and
       I feel too shy,
       but the seductive dance of the
           flickering flames before me
           burns in my stomach, and
I close my eyes;
I tilt my head, begging her summer
       breath to kiss my neck, to
       acknowledge the need
       rising in me with an expectation of release

She responds:
I feel Gaia's hands
       undress my soul and my third eye opens
       to the fullness of her body,
       to her bare flesh found on river rock;
           there are soft parts and enticing edges,
           rubbed smooth over moments spanning
           lifetimes
       by the river's sensual massage

She is so beautiful:

the roundness of her breast can be seen in the slow swaying
pines;
the practiced way she breathes on me
teases me,
it fills my imagination with promised
aromas of her wanting:
wildflowers and woodsmoke.

My third eye looks deeply into the clear waters
of a snowmelt lake and I see the depth
of her...
the unashamed, raw nudity
of her
her primal drive to make love with life
and I know we will make love in the epicenter of
my new world now shaken by desire.

The push
of her passion
is a welcomed thief;
it pushes away what remains of the inhibitions
I hide behind,
and a low growl rises to my throat
from my lust.
This excites her and the forests sing with climbing rhythms
        of the escalating breeze: trees pant,
        birdsong: low and breathy,
        flames undulate and
        humidity forms sweat on the
        sleek, silk petals of her wildflowers;
the whole of the forest edges to the slippery brink
and wanting grows.

The sound in my throat becomes a howl when I see her
lips, bit
        between the teeth of surrounding cliffs and primal
desire.
Our hands pull our bodies closer until we are
        no longer separated fleshes –
        indistinguishable by horizon or sunset, and the

sky becomes ablaze.
The air here is hot and thick like sweat,
and the rhythm of the forest grows,
mimicking my expectation.
I am in her now.

I am becoming one with her most sacred places.
I misplace my hands and any concern of gentleness.
I have no control of what pleasures I taste, but
each new bite brings me closer to the brink.
I am no longer a man.
I am beast –
made of earth, dirt and ecstacy.

She moves.
She writhes with swaying pines.
I am the rigid forest having all of her.

She moves.
She is the violent sky having all of me.
I bathe in her sap;
slip between her wildflower nectar;

She moves.
I am the river that rushes between her banks.
I am unstoppable now.
She moves.
She is the fury of wolf and prey.
I am prey.
I am volcano.
        I erupt.
I fill her with the fire she stoked within me.
She gushes and we become steam,
        evaporating into each other;
            no longer separate,
                we are the forest dance.

Discussion: Learning to Love

Love isn't just an emotion we feel. That is the easy part. Love is a verb. It is an action. It has a visible, observable state of existence.

Love is an action

I am a hopeless romantic trapped in a trauma survivor's body. Displaying emotion, or vulnerability of any kind, has always been problematic. My hurt little inner child is terrified of such vulnerabilities. It's safer to have big, thick walls up blocking people out so they won't have a chance to reject me.

But, I love so very deeply.

The problem for me wasn't about learning how to love other people, it was about learning how to be vulnerable with the emotion I felt so easily. For a long time, I learned some fake-it-till-you-make-it tricks. I knew how loving people behaved and I emulated those behaviors, because I wanted the people I loved to feel like I loved them (even though I was completely terrified of them).

There is a saying: You can't love others until you love yourself. This saying is complete bullshit. It is pure shame. The truth is that loving others (in a healthy way) is how we discover how much we already love ourselves. If we did not love ourselves, we would not be alive. The trouble is, that we don't know how to (verb/action) Love ourselves, in a healthy way. We listen to the internal trauma voices that try to convince us that we don't love ourselves or deserve love from others.

Those voices were put there by external forces. Loving is inherent.

Poetry Magic shines through my walls
The amount of love poetry I have written is certainly not reflected in this book, but this is one of my most cherished tools to circumvent the trauma walls I live with. Regardless of the type of love I feel, I can cast a poem and bleed vulnerability all over the page and I heal! And when I read it to someone, I heal! And when I stand up in front of a microphone and read to a bunch of people, I heal. And when I put my poetry into a book and share my story with others... I heal.

This kind of magic doesn't see my walls. Maybe they just see my walls for what they are: illusions. This magic cuts through them as if they were holographic.

When I use Poetry Magic as a tool for learning to Love myself and everyone/thing else, I also learn that the real magic comes from me. It is there, always waiting to be set free into the vastness of the Universe. And the supply is infinite. I'll never use it up, or run out of it.

Learning to Love is the ultimate healing
And honestly, every poem you've read in this book so far could fit into this chapter (including the ones you've cast!). My purpose for writing this book is because it is an act (verb) of Love. It is because I love myself (despite the internal trauma voices).

It is because I love you!

Practice

Now, it's your turn.

1) For this exercise, we're going to call upon the Goddess Brigid. Brigid ruled over many things, but in particular, she was the Celtic goddess of poetry. For the sake of this exercise, just know that Brigid loves you infinitely and she cherishes every aspect of you. Her arms are open and always waiting to embrace you. She is excited for every single word you write. To her, it is all poetry. Your task for this step is to sit with her, finish painting who she is to you in your mind and just sit with her.

2) When you're ready, jot down a few notes about her. Describe what she looks like. What actions does she take to make you feel loved? 3) What connections can you make between the two of you (i.e. same eyes/irises/or pupils, same favorite flower, same love of coffee, etc.).

4) When you're satisfied with your notes, cast a poem about your Love (verb) for Brigid.

5) When your satisfied with the poem you just cast, write it in the spaces provided in the next couple pages.

Thank you so much for sharing your experience with me! If you're willing, please take a photo of your poem and email it to me (warrior.poet.kmullins@gmail.com)

Chapter 6: Intuitive Poetry

Sometimes a poem exists within you that carries its own magic. I think of these poems as the Universe speaking through me using its own words. Sometimes they come up as a line that replays in my thoughts; when I put that line "on paper" the rest seems to simply fall out. These can be like living dreams that connect on a much deeper level than on the surface. If you find yourself drawn to one and you don't know exactly why, it is because you have that magic within you, and you have found connection with the Universe.

Show me Who You Are

Show me who you are,
      or explain who you are not.
Let me see what you know of you.
Let me feel your hopes and fears,
      but know that these are not you.
Are there places where
      you are not everything
            in the Universe?
Are there places you
      do not exist?

Is that chair in which you sit a chair
      because it has potential to be a chair?
Or is it a chair because you are sitting on it?
Would it be a chair if no one ever sat on it.

Do you remember at age 5 when you
      ate an apple and became the Universe?

With your first bite, you became the tree
        from which it was plucked,
        and the orchard
        and the soil.

You became the soil that nurtured life by
        the decay of death: a fallen bluebird.

You became the bluebird that once soared
        beneath the warm sunshine of Spring–
        these the same rays that filled orchards with life –
        these dreamed only for a drop of rain:
                You became the drop of rain, and
                were met with thirst and gratitude.

You remember having been a snowflake in a former life that
        fell on a distant mountain peak –
        floating, uncommitted to any particular direction.
        You melted and evaporated and
                became the clouds...

And then you became another droplet
        born by the heated thirst of young lovers...
        whose sweat from beneath an apple tree
        evaporated from quivering flesh to
        feed the clouds once more.

And you have now become these narratives,

So when I look at you,
I don't see just the version of you that
        you've become so familiar with...
I see me, because...
I remember at age five when I ate an apple...
And we became One...

Solution

*We become
solution
when material and essence coalesce,
when the apparent disparate mix,
when the mundane and the miraculous
both shine as bright,
and body and mind agree...*

*She was in love and in lust with the same person
at the same time and her sensibilities
      fought her want.
She reached to touch the stars, expecting nothing
but air and instead her flesh was burnt,
      and her sensibilities won.
Starfire could have been salvation, but
she failed a simple lesson taught by
      pocket change:
it's never enough for what you want it for,
but there's more than enough for nothing important –*

*and nothing important
is the secret to happiness.*

*She could not hear the music in the jingling change;
it sounded so much like the failings of expectation –
she missed the tones and rhythms of
      hopes and dreams.
And so, today, she died alone
sometime in the distant future
and that is why the stars weep in mourning of her
eventual passing.*

*They only sing
through the jinglings of
hopes and dreams.*

The Mountain

I had need to cross a mountain in the fourth dimension.
It was tall, but distance in the fourth dimension is suggestive only.
So, even though I could reach the top in one step,
walking is not a viable means of transportation.
Nothing is.
You see, in the fourth dimension,
kinetic energy runs inside out.
Forward motion of an object moves the entire universe
while the object stays at rest.
Have you ever tried to move a mountain?
They don't like it.
Have you ever tried to move the Universe?
It giggles like it has just been tickled.
The only way to travel in the fourth dimension
is by keeping potential energy potential, or
building intent;
They are the same thing, after all...

But there this mountain loomed beyond perceivable
visible available space.
It was purple, as deep as midnight.
There were no trees,
no plants,
no rocks,
no... dirt;
The mountain was made of Life itself.
It was a living version of a child's drawing.

I needed to climb that mountain, but
how do you intend to move but plan to not move?
It is not possible; the second makes the first a lie...
And lies are very kinetic...
Fourth dimensional mountains do not like
intentional mistruths. But I
had to find a way to the top, so
I reached inside my chest and dug
down into my solar plexus

searching for my soul and
I found an orb with my hand and
pulled it out.
It was the size of a baseball,
weighed as much as a humming bird in flight
and vibrated like laughter and confusion.
It radiated drops of inspiration that
stung when they hit my skin.
On one side of it, there was a pinhole
and I knew that if I peered inside I would see
that which I loved the most,
so I pulled the orb closer to my face and
looked inside and saw...

You...

It was you when you were seven years old...
standing alone, wearing a blue towel
on your back like a cape...
It was adorned with a hand-painted "S"
You were trying to convince yourself that you were enough,
but you never believed it...
not without some kind of super power...
not in the caged-in world you lived...

So I placed the orb near my mouth and
from the pain of love and compassion, I whispered,
"I will take you up that mountain,"
And the mountain moved toward me.
When it reached me,
the ground sliding beneath my feet began to rise
steeper as the bottom of the mountain sunk deeper behind me.
There came to me the mouth of a cave etched in the side
too small to fit my body laying down,
but when it reached me, it swallowed me and
I slid through the half-cut trench...
I was in the mountain's esophagus.

Fourth dimensional mountains eat love for nourishment.
I continued being squeezed through the cave, which swirled and turned
and wove within itself until...
I was deposited at the peak.

From the top,
I could see the entire Universe inside-out.
There were stars and planets nearby
and life was so very distant
and in the very center of it all:
a void.
I don't know why, but I threw my orb
into the void and after it landed with a "clunk"
it opened...
You flew out fiercely and immediately
commanded the Universe of the Fourth Dimension.
You were free...
jumping over skyscrapers
strong enough to fight off every fiend
I applauded you
I sang your name
I wept with joy as you stood atop your own mountain of victory
beaming confidently...

Then you looked at me and stopped...
you smiled gently and said,
"This... is how... we've always... been..."

Inhabitants of Bodies

Legs bent, as if walking;
arms
        hanging loosely,
lifeless
anticipating Death;
ankles and knees and hips creak
with the scraping of bones
                unlubricated with memories
                unpadded with experience
But bodies are unable to dwell too long in regretful
perceptions;
they turn,
        early on,
        to different paths.
It is time now
for bodies to run –
to leap – to fly...
with hope: in place of strength;
with joy: in place of comfort;
with kindness: in place of solitude.

        Sharp minds understand where
        reflections see only themselves.

And so bodies will arise and fly
through visions of mystery,
and chaos filled with beauties that come alive
        in spaces
like
words and lines
that appear broken –
they are not broken.

And bodies wear happiness like shrouds of skin
tattooed with poetry written not in words forgotten,
        but in the breath and memories lovers share

127

between
battle and embrace.
And bodies weep when uncontrolled laughter
draw constellations in the dark:
these cast spells that illuminate faces
that have come to face the dangers of
losing themselves in crowds;
they shall find solace in the ways
they wear their hopes, their joy and their kindness.

Do you remember when you discovered that
the peak of your own mountain always seemed to lie
over the next low hill on whichever path was the one you
didn't take?

Do you remember when you discovered
that it is not possible
for frozen soil to deny new growth indefinitely?

Do you remember when you discovered that
the road you actually traveled was where you truly intended
to go?

Do you remember when you discovered that
you were always just a little more than was necessary,
and gave bodies abilities to replace worry with hope.

The Trickster's

Short of breath,
     my bones have grown cold and today,
     I am weary of
     the Trickster's tactless narratives.
I have seen the tapestries of his tales;
     they are all woven from fabrics
          stripped from dreams I have when
          I should be napping, but
          remain awake:
            remembering.

I know beneath a thousand veils of fear,
     there is peace;
it glistens,
     reflecting illuminated strands of laughter
     found when mornings have been pleasant
     and afternoons have been warm:
     like when cool, mountain-spring water
     has been dried from my skin
     by suns in high altitude suns
     and green thoughts of
          new lives...

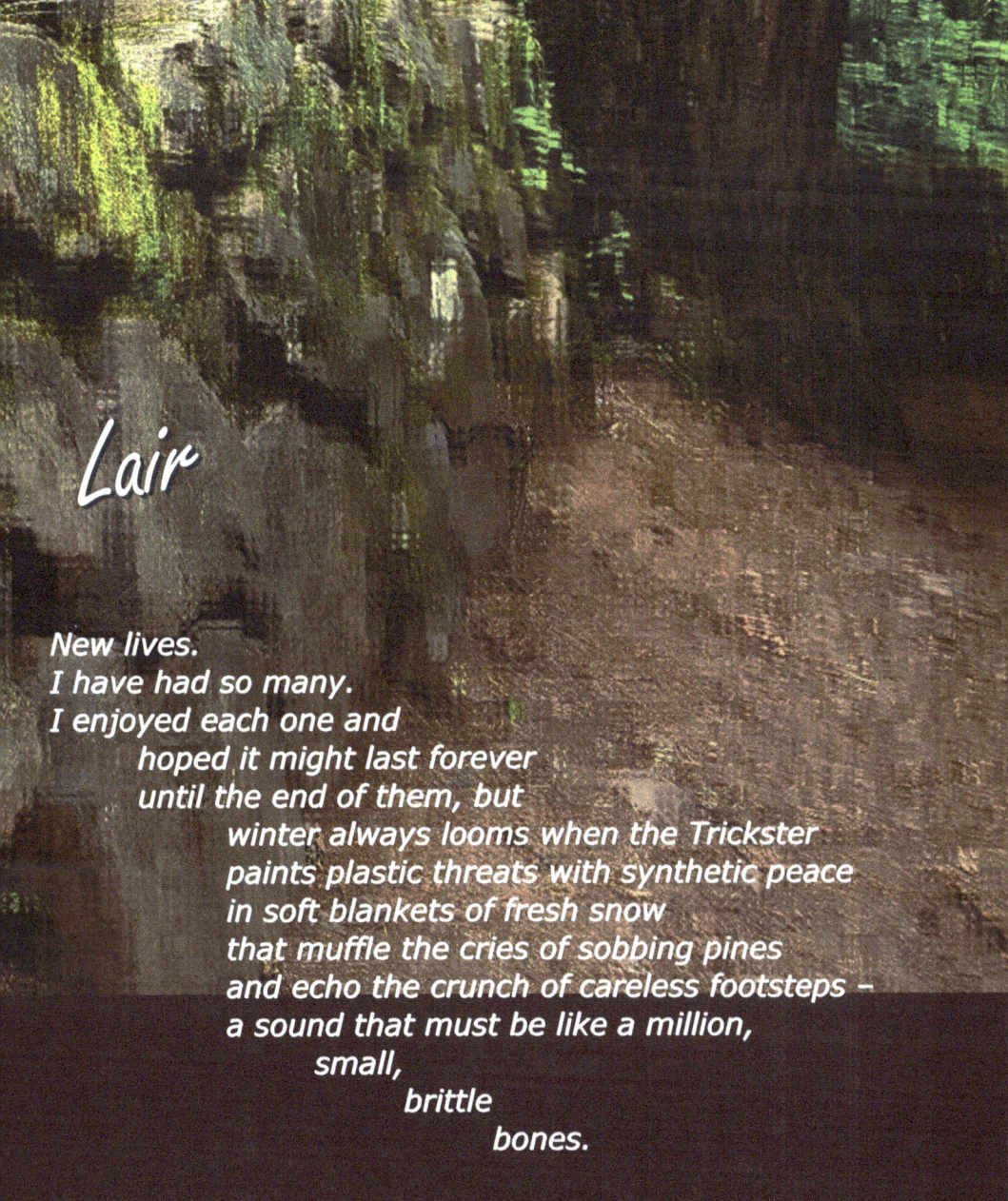

Lair

New lives.
I have had so many.
I enjoyed each one and
    hoped it might last forever
    until the end of them, but
        winter always looms when the Trickster
        paints plastic threats with synthetic peace
        in soft blankets of fresh snow
        that muffle the cries of sobbing pines
        and echo the crunch of careless footsteps –
        a sound that must be like a million,
            small,
                brittle
                    bones.

I have been here before.
I know the terrain, and how to move through it.
I remember cracks in the walls
    that function like ladders
    for when I'm ready
    to climb out into the fresh air once again.
Don't worry,
    the Trickster will not be my
        belayer.

Rumi tells me that those cracks are where the light comes in.
I am alone here and I would paint
        pieces of this place with the
        fragments of his narratives,
but the Trickster mixes
paints too thin and colors come
out looking too much like sadness:
the blues become forced smiles;
the greens become silt picked up by
gentle disturbances;
the whites are not innocence,
        they are
                naiveté.

This is not sadness though, and
smiles here are genuine
        as are the tears...
What looks like silt is nothing more than
careless judgment and
        naiveté is not the same shade as
                ignorance.
So, I am alone, but I'm not lonely.
The Trickster is here with me.
I watch as he plays hide and seek by himself.
I don't bother picking up brushes, but
seek to confront him in my reflection
where I know I will not find him.
But, that is the only place I have look?
Can I find him in his own narratives?
Does he spill his secrets all over himself?
When I look at him,
        I see my self-perception;
                when I look away,
                I see my
                        self.

We Are Winter

And we were Winter –
necessary and detested –
but we knew we would become Spring.

Need hides from sight by
cold and snow and nights so long
They feel like finding the end of a story
    somewhere in the middle.

We have been there, though,
where stars sing and dance:
    whether there are cloud blankets or not;
    whether the atmosphere is crisp and clear
        or quiet in fear;
    whether those we've known have come or gone;
        or stayed awhile by our fires;
    whether or not we've felt alone or lonely
        in solitudes we've made or
        solitudes we've bartered with.

And we were Spring –
anticipated and welcome –
but we knew we would become Summer.

And our eyes will open to the Sun –
    as if we expected warmth –
    and we will fly across the skies
        on hubris and wax wings.
We will stretch across the new expanse of days –
    each one filled with
more minutes than
yesterday;
Like them, we too will be more than we were
    yesterday
    opening to quiet voices singing psalms
        of new growth

and love poems.

And we were Summer –
bare-skinned and bone-dry –
but we knew we would become Autumn.

And the soles of our feet will sketch the sand
like visions envisioned but still invisible
lines of Poetry that trail along the edge of the page
but not being long enough to fill with love.

We will rest under a Sun that
loses track of time and
shines too long for evening's pride.
We won't feel guilt for lingering there in ease;
it is not the fault of hot days
that stars become lazier.

And we were Autumn –
expected and awaited –
but we knew we would become Winter.

And we waited on the edge of the growing night sky
where the winds would wish to blow:
we fell out of our heights from grace
and drifted slowly to the ground.

We discovered beauty in our demise
and wished for the caress of our Great Mother;
she would cherish us and remake us
in one of her multitude of images.

And we are Winter but we know we will become
Spring.

133

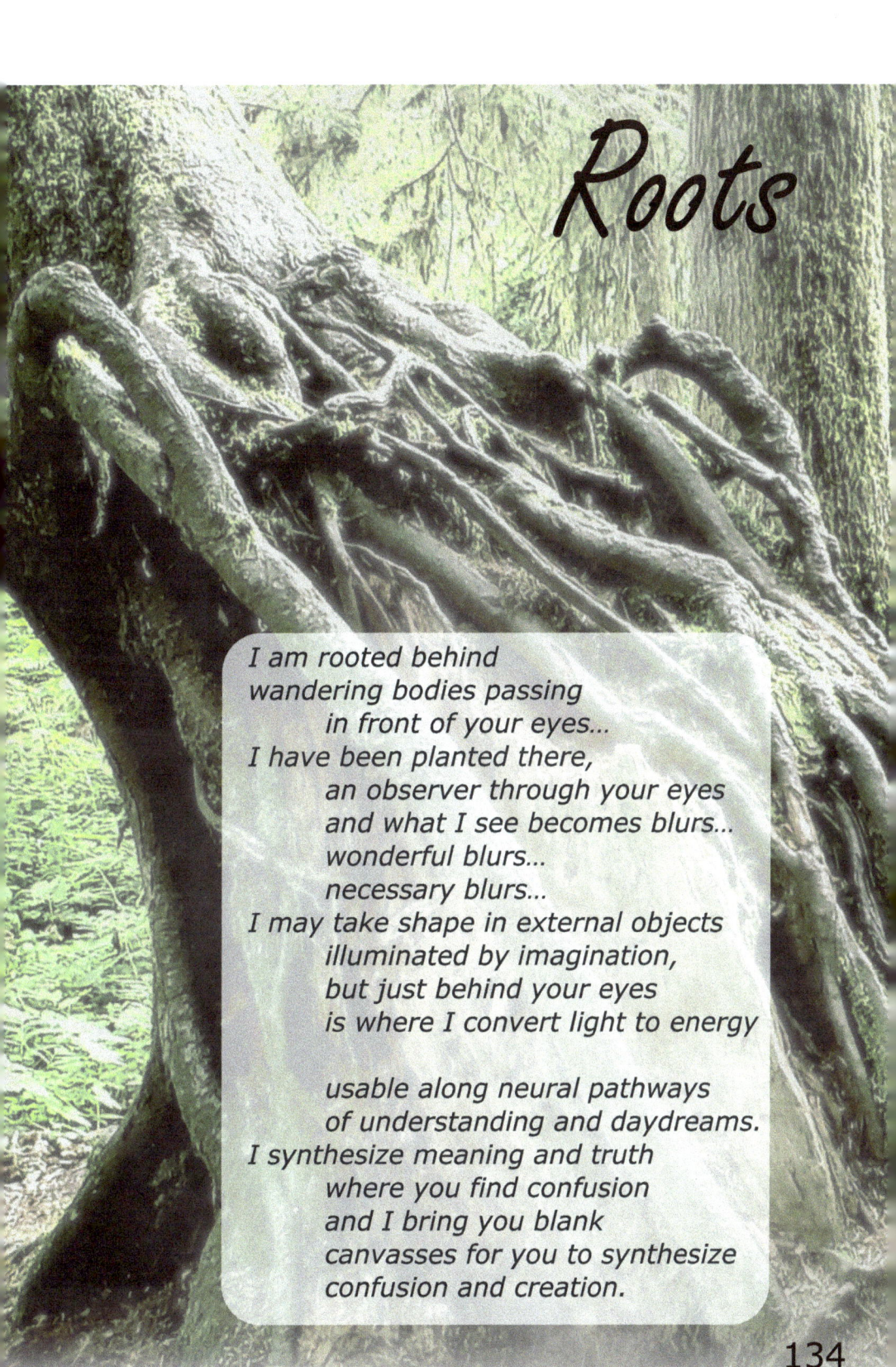

Roots

I am rooted behind
wandering bodies passing
    in front of your eyes...
I have been planted there,
    an observer through your eyes
    and what I see becomes blurs...
    wonderful blurs...
    necessary blurs...
I may take shape in external objects
    illuminated by imagination,
    but just behind your eyes
    is where I convert light to energy

    usable along neural pathways
    of understanding and daydreams.
I synthesize meaning and truth
    where you find confusion
    and I bring you blank
    canvasses for you to synthesize
    confusion and creation.

Wish for me to soar and
        I will paint your imagination
on the clouds.
Ask me to swim within the crests of the biggest waves and
you will see
me soaking beneath blue waters,
laughing with merfolk
        to slow streams of whalesong.
Ask me to walk and
        you will find me strolling along
                mountain peaks effortlessly
                plucking pine cones from the ground
                        like fibonacci fruits
                        that look too much like
                        sweet, sticky galaxies.
Wish for me to be free and
        you will find me smiling
                in the constant conversation
                you and I have been having since
                        the dawn of eternity...

I have been here rooted within you,
        and I am glad
        for your creations.

keep looking...
keep seeing...
keep creating...

Solitude

My lips part, but my lungs are deflated.
Who would hear me?
I've held my breath for so long, there's nothing left of words but
dust.
I walk, and my footsteps echo long replies...
Darkness is interrupted by moonlight reflections
on cold tile polished by expectation and fear;
windows are too high to see anything but the most distant stars.
This is an endless hallway.
I am walking the length of an infinite needle
but never reach the point.
So I walk slowly through filtered moonbeams and sometimes
hear the hallway speak to me:
Clip, clop, Clip, clop...
I'm not lost, but I don't know where I'm going...

There are doors from time to time.
I stop to check them, but they're almost always locked tight.
So tight they do not budge, nor rattle when I shake them with
my pleas for something new.
Sometimes they are only painted on.

But sometimes they open.

The first one I found in this condition revealed a small white

room:
white floor, white walls, a white ceiling.
In the center of the room is a white chair and there is nothing else.
Light fills every space.
Where beautiful grey shadows should be, there was only more white.
I sat in the chair and the door closed behind me, sealing perfectly in its frame,
with no features to distinguish it from the wall.
There were no echoes in this room.
There were no sounds.
I meditated with my eyes open and mind painted technicolor pictures in my periphery.
My eyes would chase them, but they would disappear.
The world I could not look at became incorrect hues
of shapes distorted but alive...
I wanted something to be real, but
none of it was
When I became disinterested, the door opened,
and I went back into the hallway, godless.

Clip, clop, clip, clop...

The second unlocked door revealed a brightly colored room.
In the middle of the room, there was a soft couch and a low table.
On the table was a wine glass filled with a green liquid.
A small card leaned against the glass.
I took my shoes and socks off and tread across thick carpet,
which tickled the soft parts of my foot.
I sat in the couch and read the card,
"Drink me, and I'll drink you"
I took a sip.
My tongue was washed in burning sweetness sliding down my throat.
Passion lining my esophagus made my mind go numb.
My body trembled and I lost control of my extremities.
Fingers traced my jaw, hands squeezed my shoulders, claws scratched my back,
teeth bit my lip...
I was lost to pleasure.

137

But only for a moment before it passed,
To be replaced with anxiety
and so I took another sip.
This time, there was no flavor.
There was no odor.
The color in the room faded to mocking shadows.
I ran across the carpet, now matted and stained and filled with grit,
to my hallway.
I left that room fearing that what I desired wanted me dead.

Clip, clop, clip, clop...

The third door opened to a hall of mirrors.
At first, they were sporadic,
they transformed my body into silly shapes.
I laughed at each one and moved on to the next.
I continued until the laughter turned to sobs and I could no longer see.
I could not tell how large this room was, but it seemed to go on forever.
The deeper in I traveled, the reflective forest thickened.
Panic filled every reflection.
Copies of me occupied every odd angle.
All reflected eyes penetrated comfort zones or
denied me altogether as if I were a distorted reflection...
I have never before felt so examined.
As mirrors became so packed together, stress formed cracks
I could hear faint creaking sounds, threatening to shatter.
My panic raged...
I wanted out...
I could not find my way...
One step more and all mirrors shattered.
Billions of me fell to the floor.
I became a blizzard;
no two shards of me were the same...
And when all of me lay in mirror dust, a new door became revealed...
I waded through the glittering shards –
unaware of the blood flowing from my feet –
my path behind me mapped with every injury...
The door pulled open effortlessly and I leapt through without

thinking.
I fell to the floor and found it odd my wounds never existed.
I was back in my hallway and that door turned out to be painted
on
so I began to walk again...

Clip, clop, clip, clop...

The fourth door hid a small closet.
Inside, there was an empty bucket.
It had never been used, and had collected no dust.
There were two shelves:
one contained nothing
one contained a plain, unadorned, glass cup, a matching plate,
and simple utensils
ready to serve a meal I knew would never exist.
They were empty.
They were clean.
I closed the door and remained in my hallway.
There was no room for me in that closet

Clip, clop, clip, clop...

The fifth door.
A living room.
A couch, reclining chairs, coffee table, end tables, lamps, a
television.
On the couch holding a remote control a mannequin.
She wore a plastic smile.
A bowl of plain potato chips sat on her lap untouched.
On the table, a dusty plastic rose bouquet, an undealt deck of
cards, and an unlit stick of incense.
I entered the room and sat on the couch next to the mannequin.
I took my shoes off and put my feet on the coffee table.
My socks were clean and bleached.
I placed my hand on the mannequin's knee and stared at the
television screen until I fell asleep.
I do not know how long I slept, but when I woke up, I was old.
My skin was loose and weathered.
I stood and every joint creaked with pain.
I walked to a mirror hanging on the wall.
There was a face I did not recognize.

139

I did not know what to do with it.
I tried to stretch out unfamiliar lines, but when I let go, they returned.
I sought comfort in the blank gaze of mannequin's glassy eyes,
but they could see nothing beyond the television screen
and I knew if I didn't get out I would die this way,
So I shuffled to the door and back into my hallway.

Clip, clop, clip, clop...

And there was one final door.
A set of gilded, carved, double doors slightly ajar –
mirrored flames carved on the doors –
aromas of good food cooking wafting through the opening...
I approached and peered inside
It was a kitchen,
There was a man there, and it was me....
His brow was wet with perspiration...
He hunched and looked forlorn...
A beautiful woman stood with her back to him...
small ghostly demons orbited her head at dizzying speeds
screaming at her...
mangled faces belittling her...
They tried to speak through her mouth.
She turned producing a handful of oranges
She looked at me and screamed,
"I don't have any apples to give you!"
The other version of me whispered hopelessly,
"He doesn't want apples."
I turned around looking for escape and the lobby was gone...
So I walked quietly through the double doors and the other me
noticed my entrance, smiled and said,
"Welcome home... please," he begged, "let me show you to the
exit..."

Clip, clop, clip, clop...

My hallway reached an abrubt end:
a solid wall and nothing more.
No more doors.
I was done.
I stopped.

I looked behind me down my hallway, and as I stood there,
        it remained unchanging.
However, as I examined my current occupied location,
everything began to change.
Moonlight danced on floor and wall
(from where, I cannot say)
and as I moved my body, my perspective,
shadows and moonlight became pallet and paint...
I became the canvass and, as I danced, for kaleidoscope-hope
painted all over my body;
I examined all my hallway's walls in this current location and
found beautiful cracks in paint –
fine, delicate cracks, like hair on a newborn...
Around the cracks, the concrete became soft enough that I could
scrape away concrete crumbs and rub cement dust onto the old
tile floor
and write poetry in it with my finger.
I turned a crack in the wall into a hole and for the first time since I
began this journey,
I could peer out into the world outside.
I was surprised to find a world outside.
It was lush and beautiful and alive and growing...
I dug and pulled and rammed my shoulder into the wall until it
came crashing down.
I stood tattered and bruised amid a pile of debris, but I could feel
the warmth
of my face in sunlight that illuminated a meadow so pleasant that
I could not imagine not wanting to lay in it for eternity...
And just before I prepared to step out onto the lawn,
I took another look back down the hallway I had spent a lifetime
walking...
It was not a hallway,
but just another room,
a lobby...

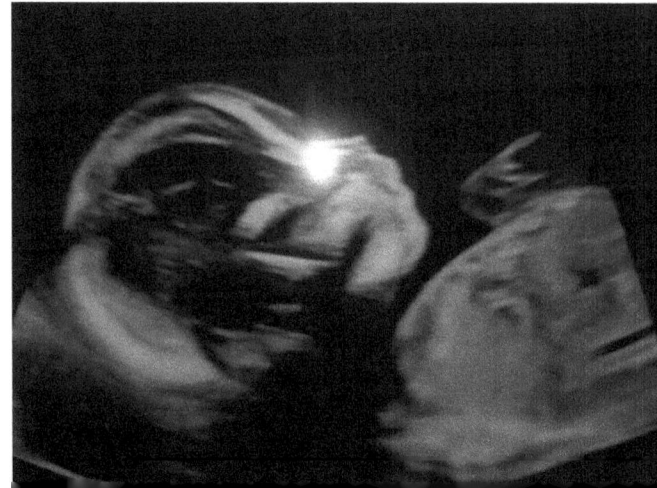

Discussion: Intuitive Poetry

There is a rune sometimes used by readers that is blank. Sometimes it is called Wyrd, which means fate or destiny. Wyrd could be interpreted as, "there is no answer." But I think it means that the answer is not for our conscious minds, but for our intuitive minds.

The gods can't do everything for us!

Intuitive poetry is simple. I don't have a lot to say about it except that we let our inner voice write it for us. So, we're not going to delay and just jump write into...

Practice

1) Do your best to sit in a comfortable position, ready to write. Like, lazy comfortable. Just relax.
2) Let your mind drift and your thoughts run free. Close your eyes if it helps.
3) Listen to your thoughts. As carefully as you can.
4) Eventually, you'll get a thought/idea that just falls somewhere on the spectrum of bizarre.
Write it down. This is your prompt.
5) Now, just let your words flow. Just don't stop writing. Keep your prompt in mind, but let your words drift from it if they need to. Let them stop when they want to.
6) When you're satisfied with the poem you just cast, write it in the spaces provided in the next couple pages.

Thank you so much for sharing your experience with me! If you're willing, please take a photo of your poem and email it to me
(warrior.poet.kmullins@gmail.com)

FIN

My Last Cast

We started this book talking about what Poetry Magic is. Let's end the book talking about what Poetry Magic does.

Poetry magic makes connections. It connects us with our higher self and our base self. It connects us with our past and our future... and especially our present. it connects us with our friends, family, acquaintances, and even our enemies. It connects us with our hopes and fears, fantasies and realities, and our dreams and our goals. It connects us with the way the sun shines through that flower petal, and beads of dew on that spider web.

Poetry Magic connects us with the Universe. Whatever that feels like to you. The Universe is infinite. You are a piece of the Universe. A little part of infinity, is infinity. Therefore, you are infinite. You are the Universe.

Please, feel your heart with your soul, right now. Listen to the choir of angelic voices in the distance and embrace all that Poetry Magic has to offer you.

I cast the poems contained within this book over many years and each one brought me a little closer to this truth. And now my time with this work has come to an end, but the work has really only just begun.

Following, if you haven't already seen, are many pages of space for you to write. Please, continue to cast your beautiful Poetry Magic on those pages and let this work live yet. And share your work every chance you can: to individuals, groups, open mics, poetry readings, anywhere (including me, please: warrior.poet.kmullins@gmail.com).

If we heal ourselves, we heal others, we heal the world. And this poor world needs us.

Thank you for sharing this journey with me.

Boomer's Prayer

I love you!
And you deserve all the Love there is in the Universe!
All there is to have,
and all there is to give.
You deserve it not because of what you've done, but
because of who you are...
At the moment of Creation, the Universe sought
all of Infinity forthe best being to be you
There were infinite possibilities across all of time and all of
space and
you were the perfect choice.
None could be better!
You deserve all the Love in the Universe because...
you are you...
You are Love!

Acknowledgments

This project has been a lifetime in the making. The poetry contained within comes from my experiences, traumatic, tragic, joyous, and beautiful. My gratitude extends to all my abusers and all my loves and I will do my best here to acknowledge all of the most important relating to this project.

First, me. At the time of this writing, I am homeless (for almost a year now) and living in a tent. After a series of tragic and traumatic events between early November and late December 2021, I found myself discharged from a two-week stay at a mental hospital for suicidality. After being released, I found myself alone in a strange town, states away from what had been my home most of my life. I did not know a single person. It was me, my dog, and my Chevy Tahoe. I endured. I am enduring. Through it all, I now sit here with an incredible support network, friends I love and who love me, a job supporting people with disabilities, and this book you hold.

I am a miracle of the Universe. And so are you!

Now then, here are the people important to me and to this project.

Brenda and Robbie have been my biggest cheerleaders in my daily life and in this project. Without their material, mental, emotional, and spiritual support, I can honestly say you would not be reading these words. Thank you both for being who you are! I love you eternally!

This would not have been possible without my backers from Kickstarter who funded the making of this book: Jerald Wegehenkel, Brenda Bonesteel, Shannah Eichel, Selene, Ashlee Nunez, L.S, Anna McCluskey, Brian Finley, Robert, Andy Van Brocklin, Nathan Greensweight, Briana Foster, Zachary Pettit, Jodi Gill, Sarah Orr Aten.

These people (or entities) also support me personally in ways that are

191

much much bigger than the time, aid and words they gift to me (some are duplcates from the above list): Ashlee, Mandy, Sydnee, Aubrey, Matt, Angie, Dawn, Jay, Scott P., Leslie S., Joy, Terran, Team OIP, Emily B., Chris and Brandi, Frank, Emily M., my Mom and Keith, my Sissifer, Courtenay, Patrik H., Katelyn, Will N., Jeramie, Jodi and Jonathan, Jenna H., Helenna, James, Gena K.S., Kelly L., Amanda and TJ, Megan, Kevin, CHANCE Recovery, the Ecstatic Dance community, Poetics Corvallis, my Bozeman Poetry Collective crew, David, Kimberly, and many more I hope to remember before this goes to print.

I would like to extend a special thank you to Jolene for being such an amazing, loving and wise Mom to my children.

If you desire to publish your own book, consider using the following open source softwares: OpenOffice.org (like MS Office, but better), and Scribus (page-layout software). These are free. They have a learning curve, but active and vibrant communities that have already answered every question under the sun! Save yourself some money and support these important projects.

Finally, I want to thank the Universe. In the vastness of your infinity, you chose me to be me. Your sense of humor isn't great, most of the time. While my life has been filled with more traumas than seems fair for one person, you've carried me through everything safely. Thank you for the gifts that have molded me into who I am. Thank you for teaching me every day how to love. Thank you for the person reading this right now!

www.ingramcontent.com/pod-product-compliance
Lightning Source LLC
Chambersburg PA
CBHW051618120626
46551CB00014B/1854